Dorit Dror – Painter

Published by: Yotzrim Art Gallery - Consulting and selling art
Design: Roni oz

© All rights reserved to Yotzrim Art Gallery - Consulting and Sale of Art- 2020
www.yotzrimgallery.com

Address: PO Box 5123, Herzliya, ZIP Code 4649719
Phone: +972-54-5286808

Do not reproduce, copy, photograph, record, translate, store in a database, transmit or receive in any way or transmit data from it in any form or electronic means, optical or mechanical or otherwise - any part of the material in this book. Commercial use of any kind of material contained in this book is strictly prohibited without the prior permission of the creators of the gallery.

Dorit Dror
Painter

Dorit Dror was born in kibbutz Hefziba Israel in 1950. She now lives and works in KFAR JONA near TEL AVIV. Dorit has graduated the "Bet Berl school of art" and specialist in glass work as well as drawing and painting. Dorit draws her inspiration from her life experience and her work and preforms by dialog between the art of photography and drawing.

Her work is vibrant with brush strokes heavy texture and a level of realism that people like.

She knows how to abstract the background so the main subjects stand out better.

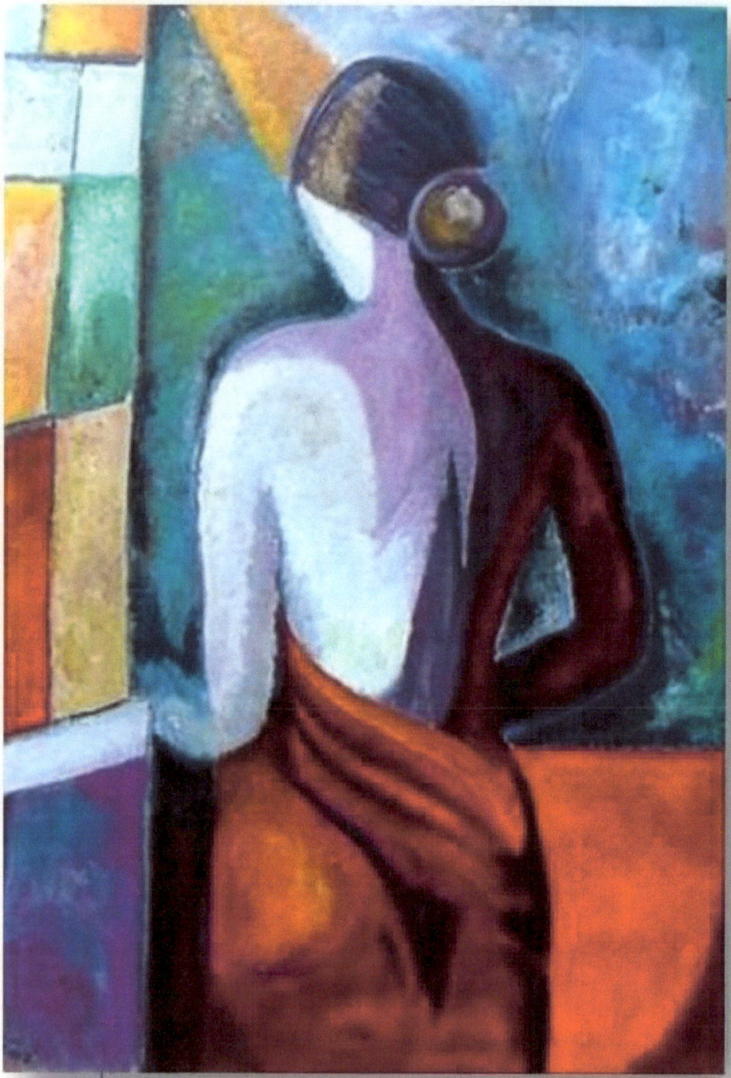

Oil on canvas, 60 by 50 cm

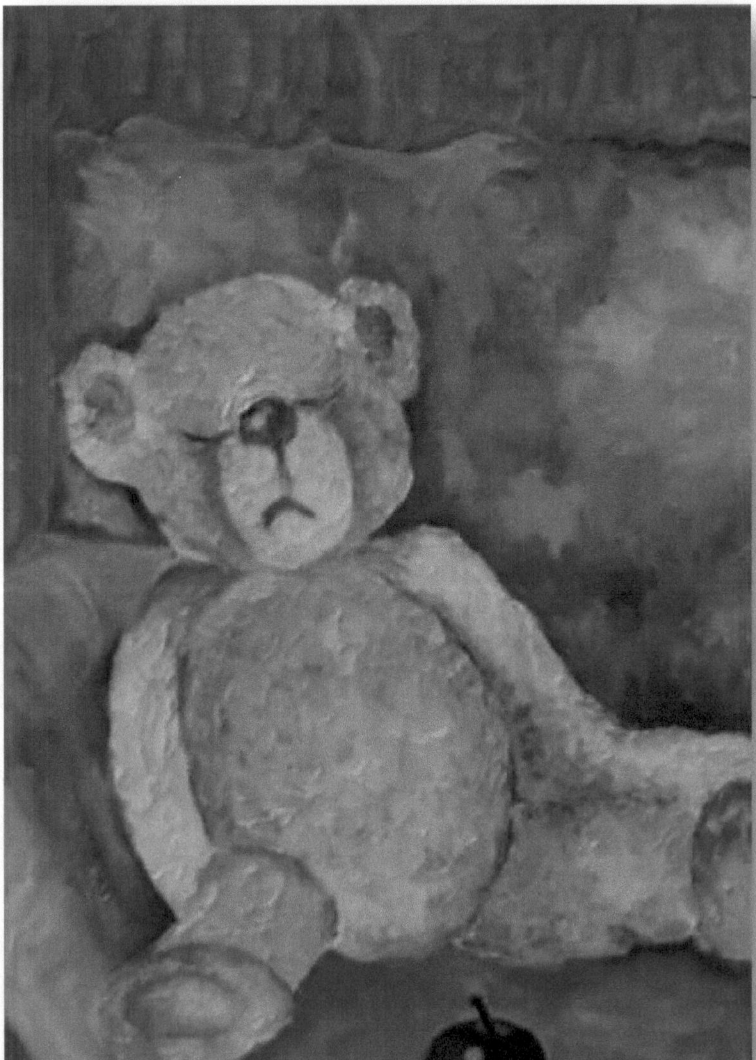

Oil on canvas, 50 by 35 cm

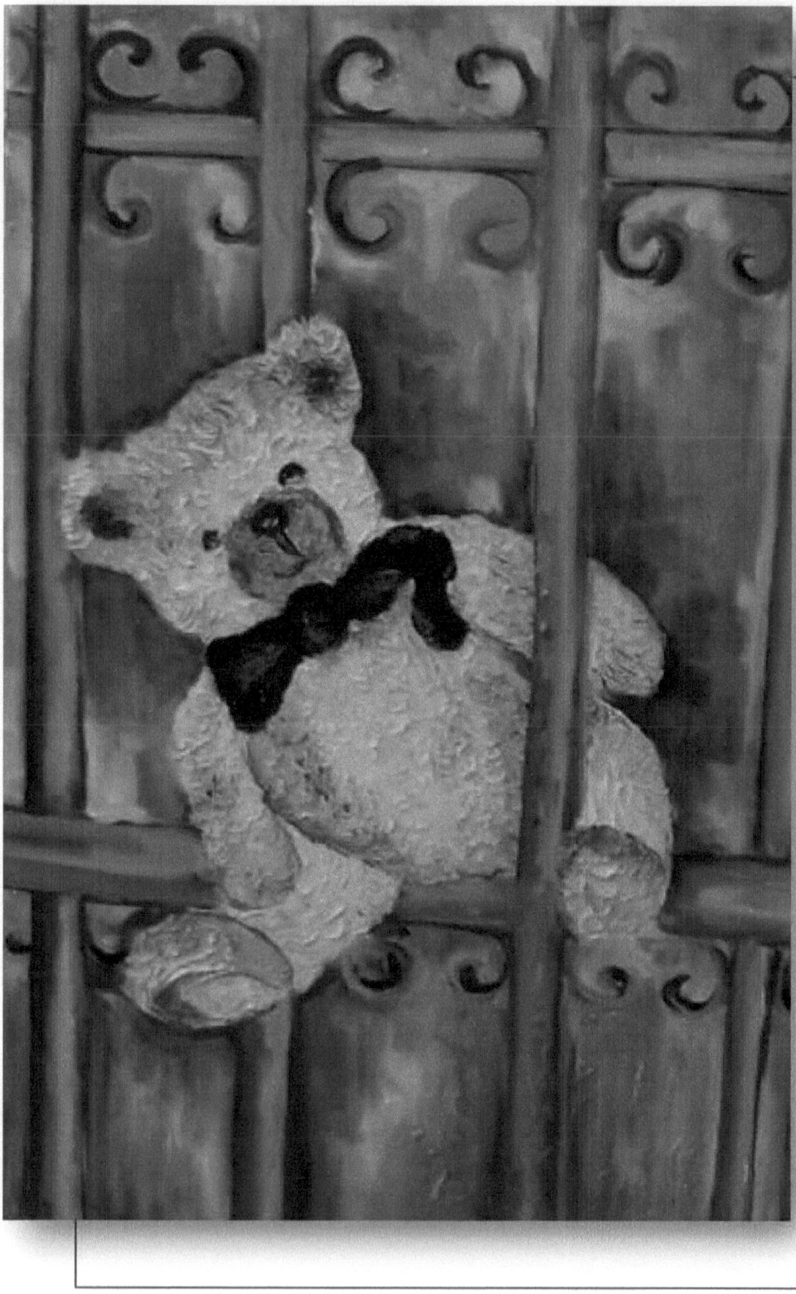

Oil on canvas, 35 by 50 cm

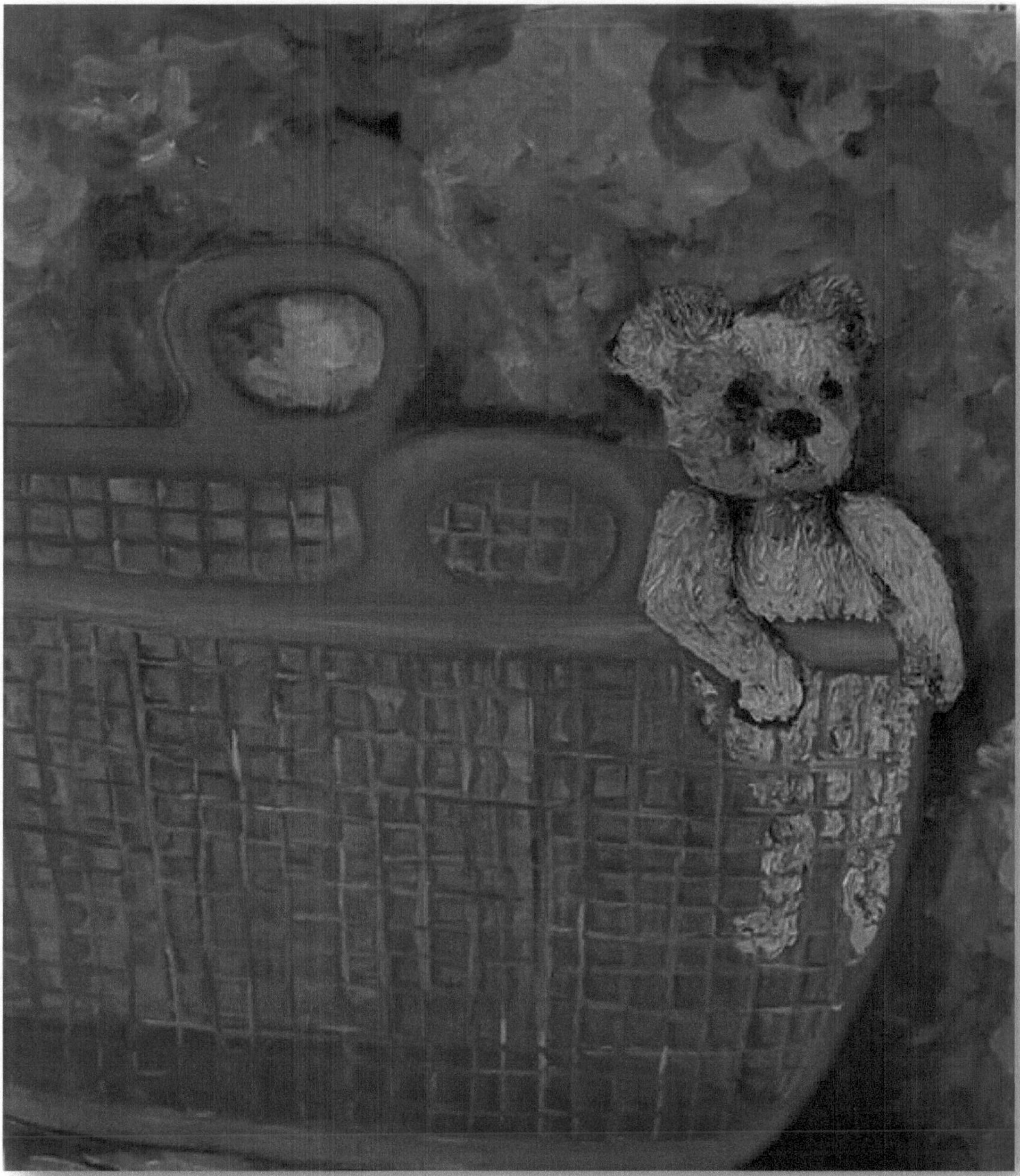

Oil on canvas, 40 by 40 cm

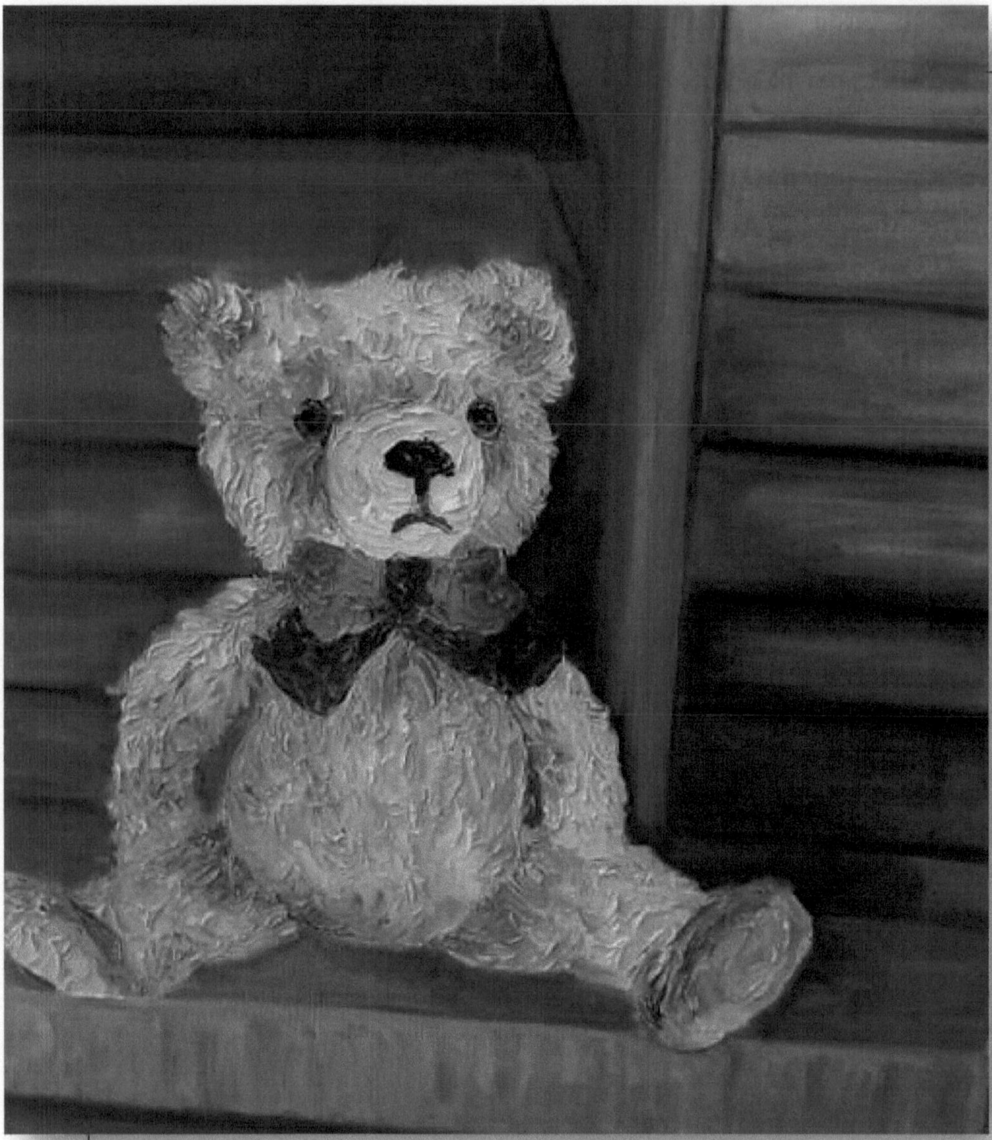

Oil on canvas, 40 by 40 cm

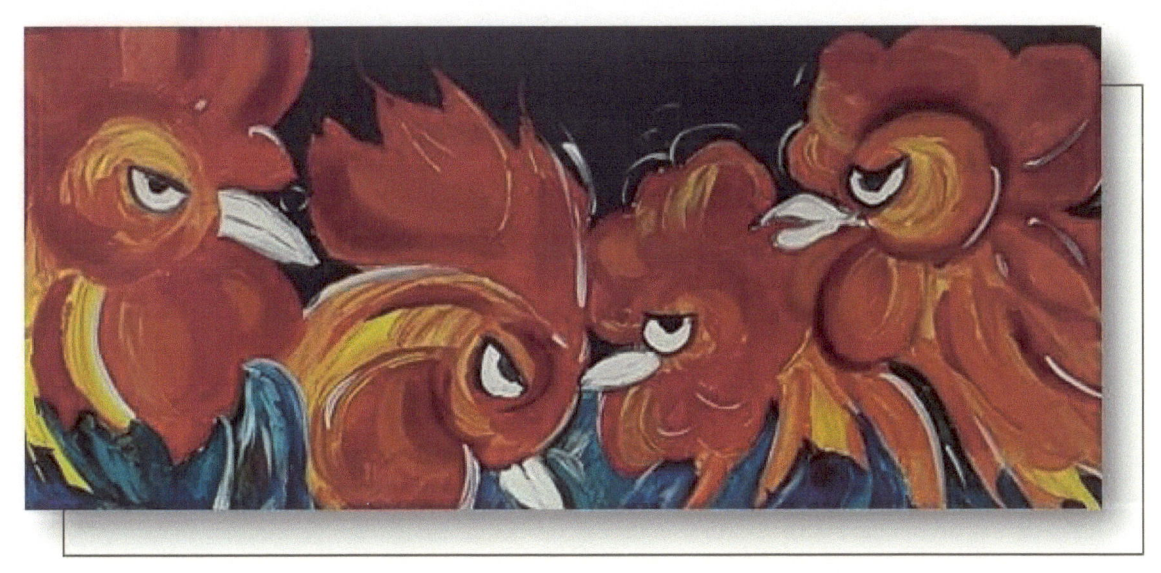

Oil on canvas, 40 by 100 cm

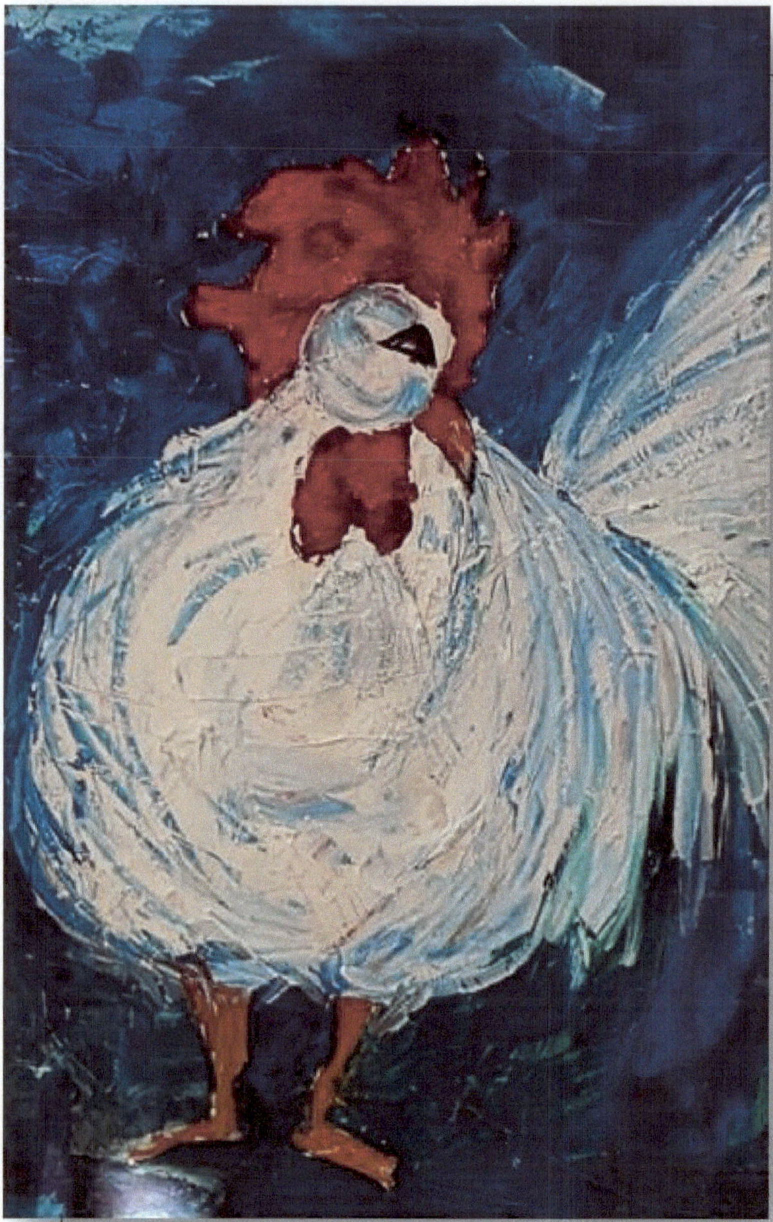

Oil on canvas, 50 by 40 cm

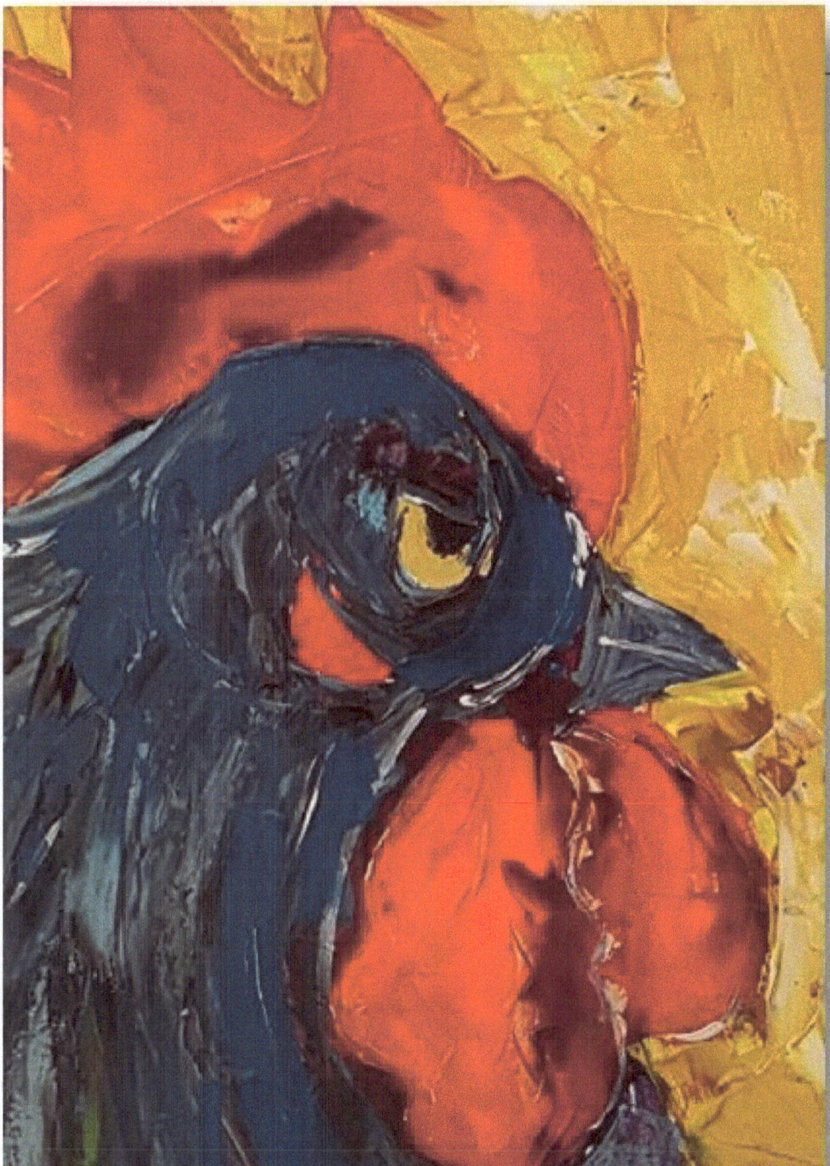

Oil on canvas, 60 by 45 cm

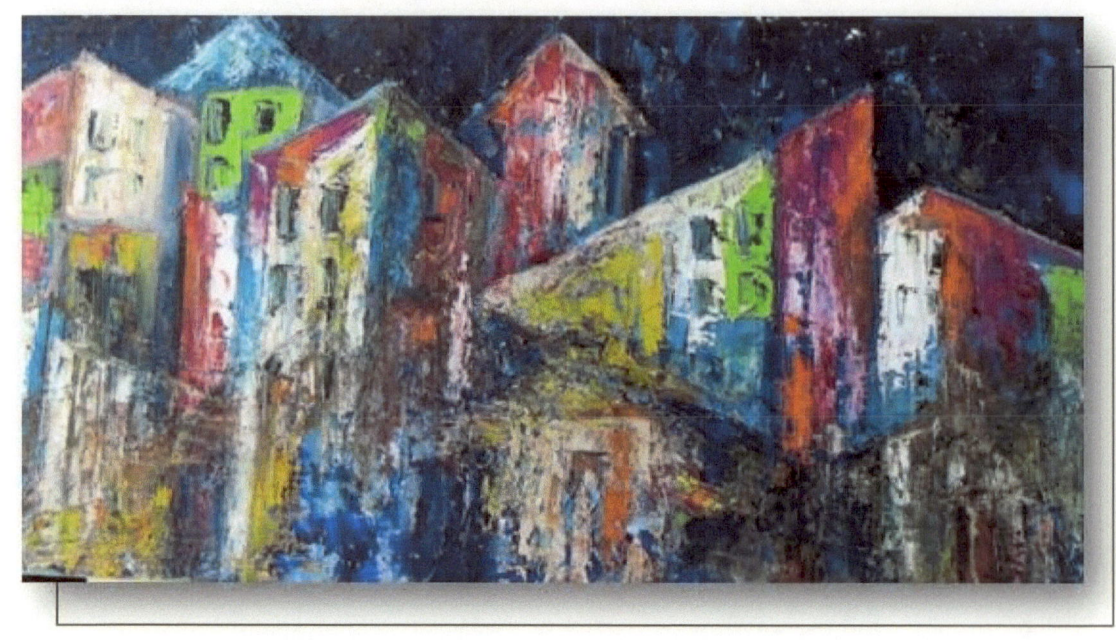

Oil on canvas, 40 by 100 cm

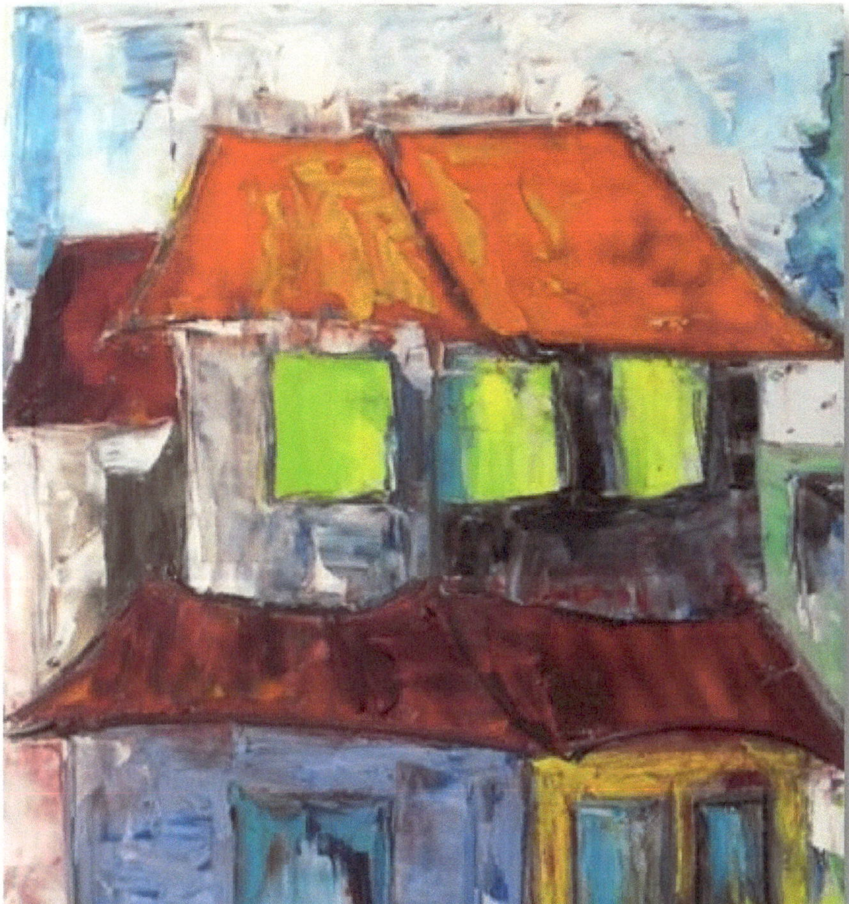

Oil on canvas, 50 by 40 cm

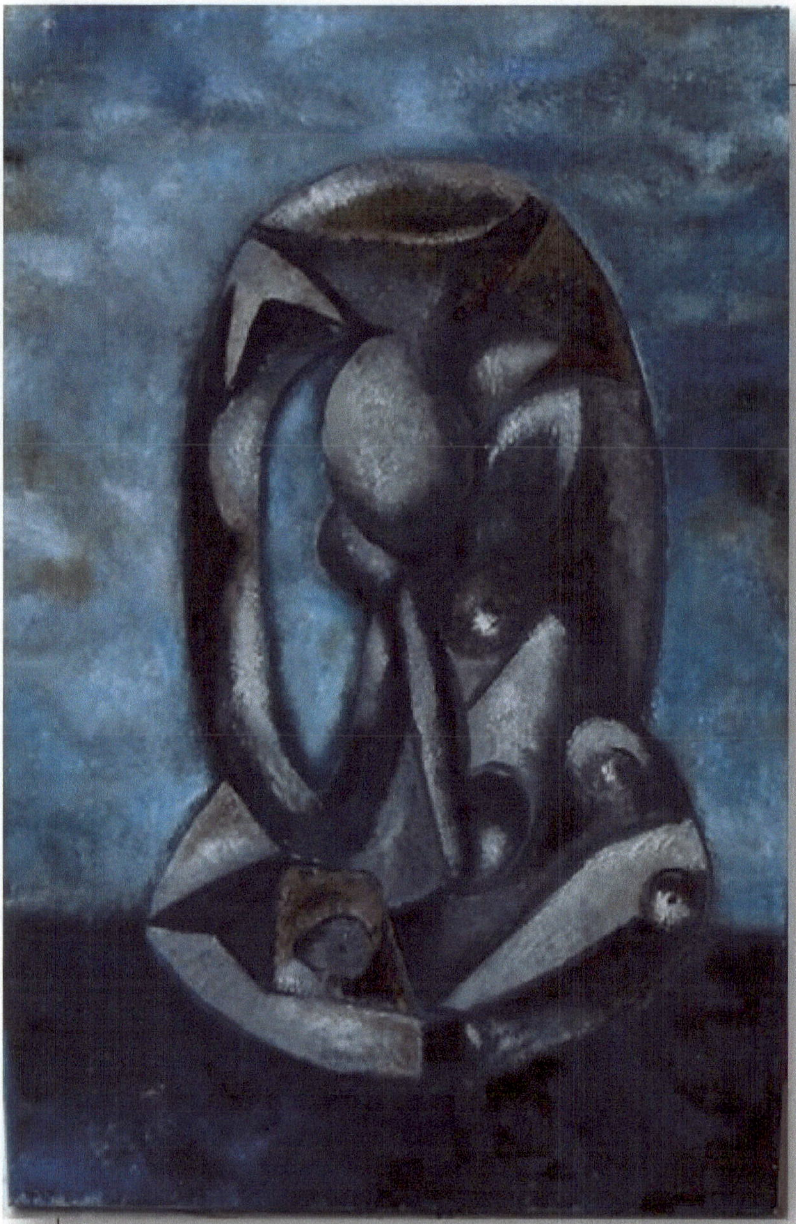

Oil on canvas, 50 by 35 cm

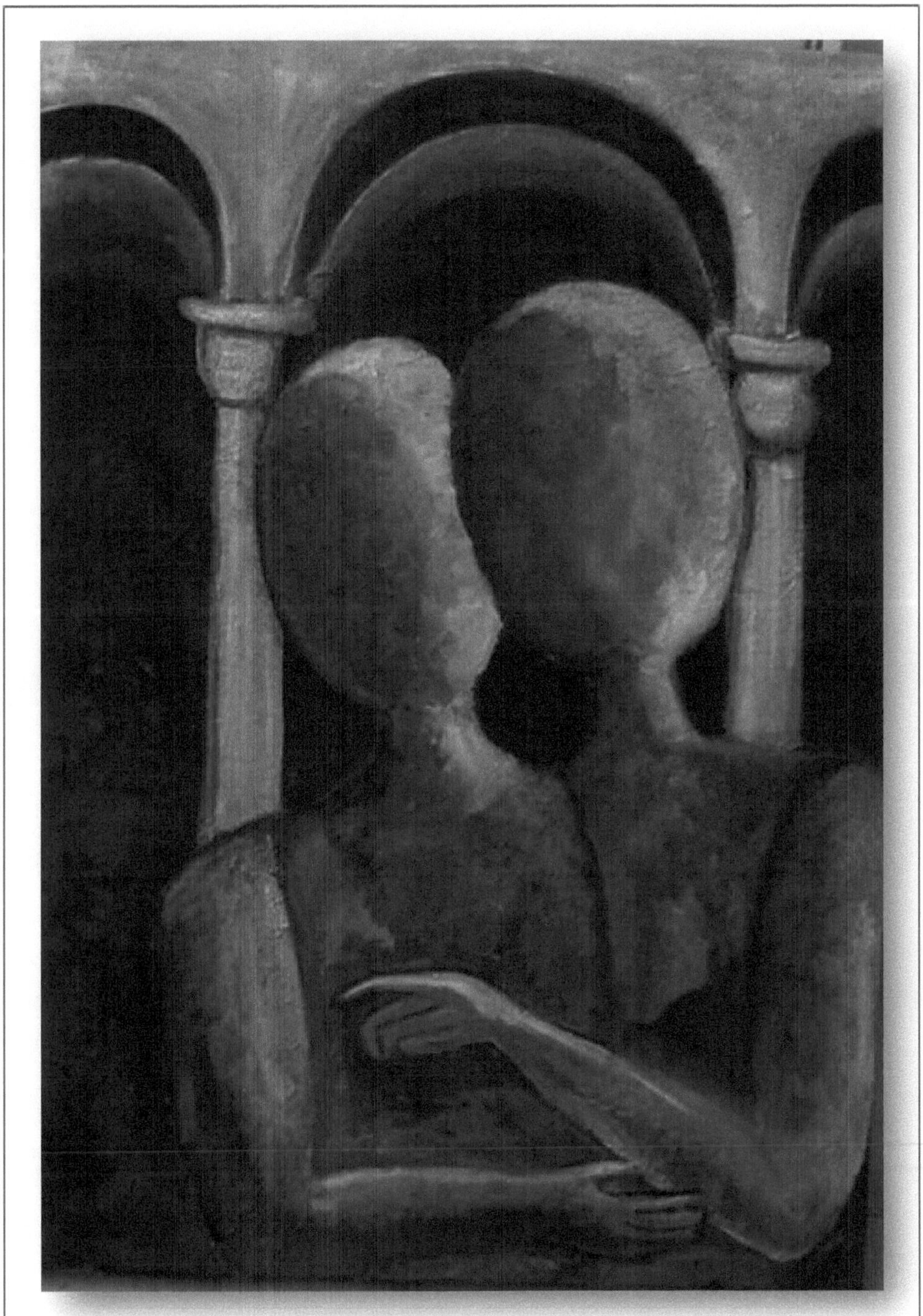

Oil on canvas, 60 by 50 cm

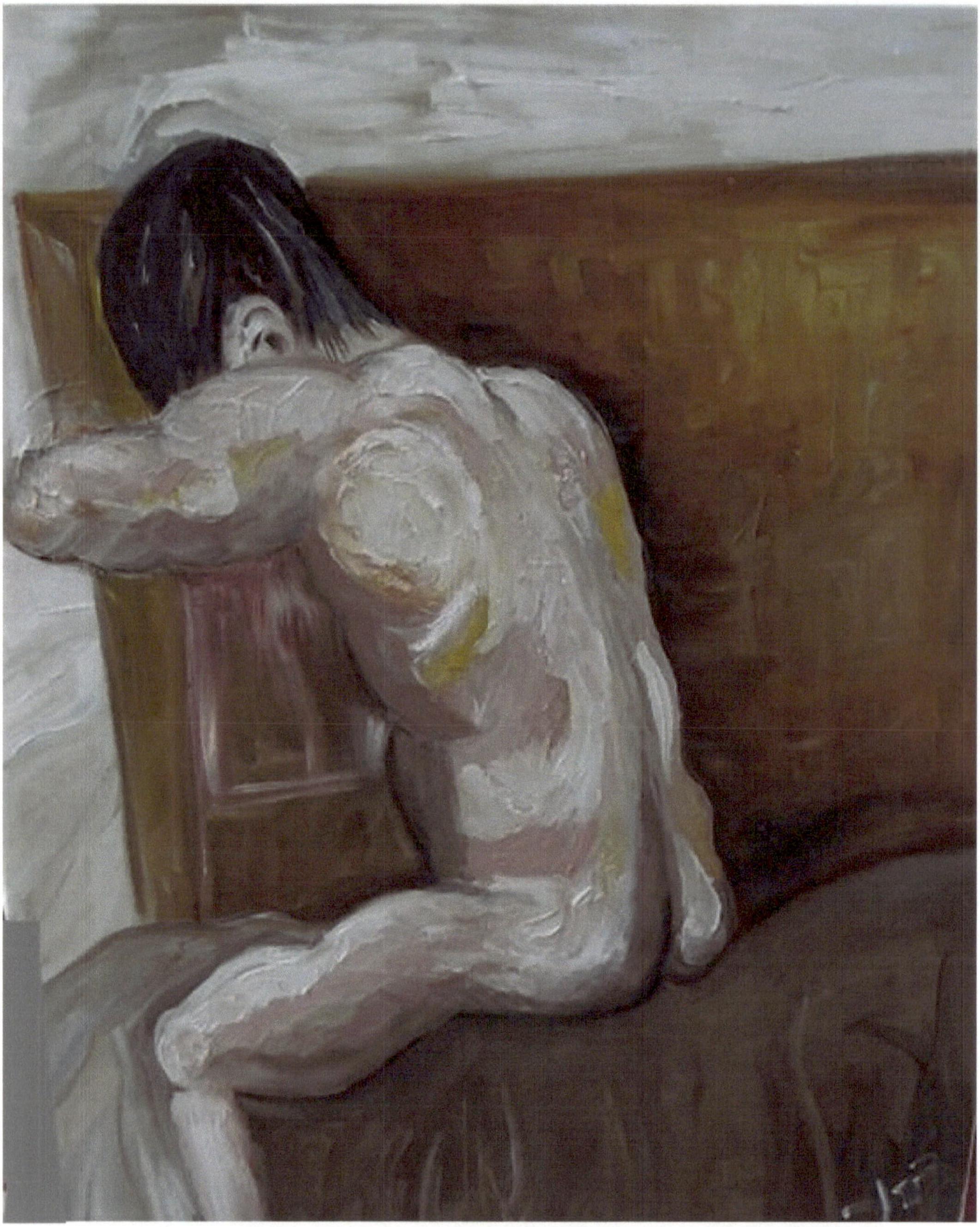

Oil on canvas, 50 by 40 cm

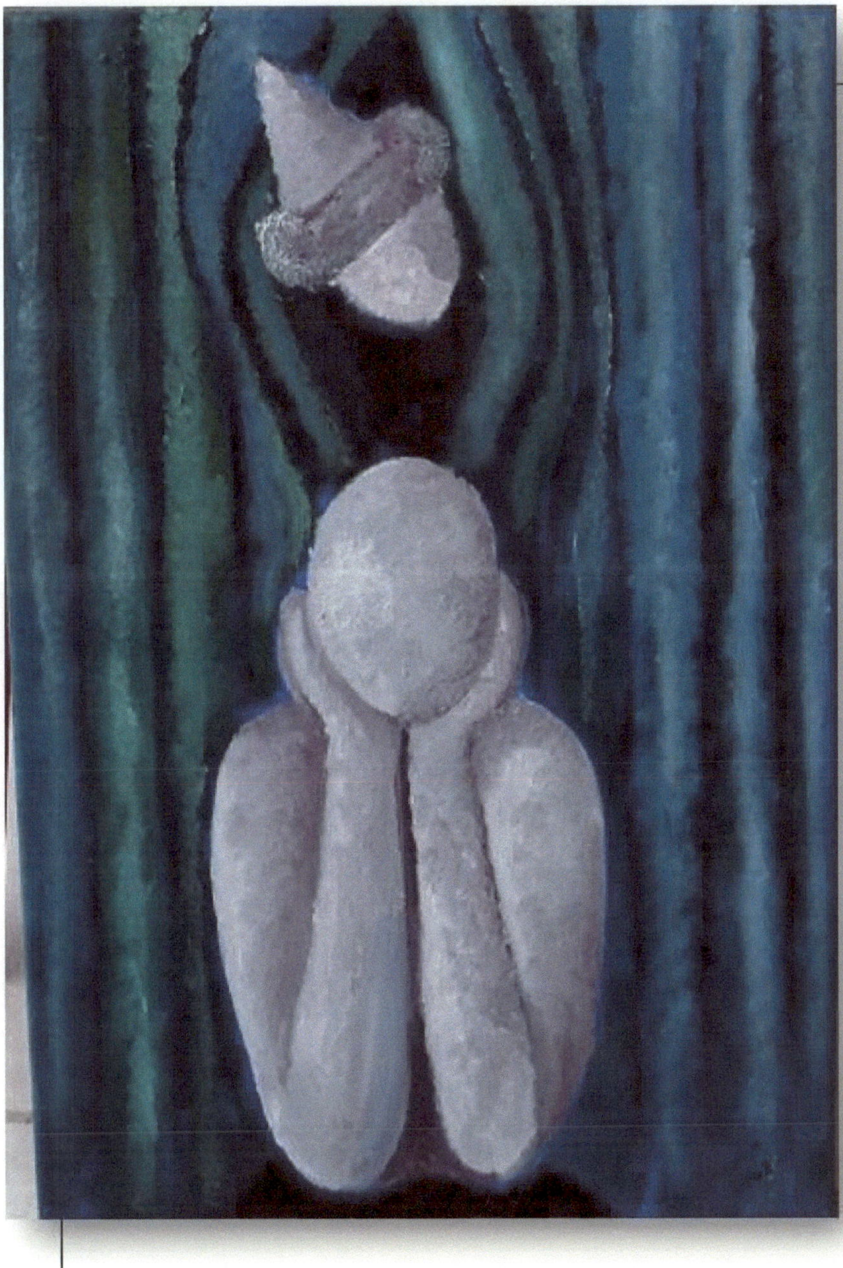

Oil on canvas, 45 by 40 cm

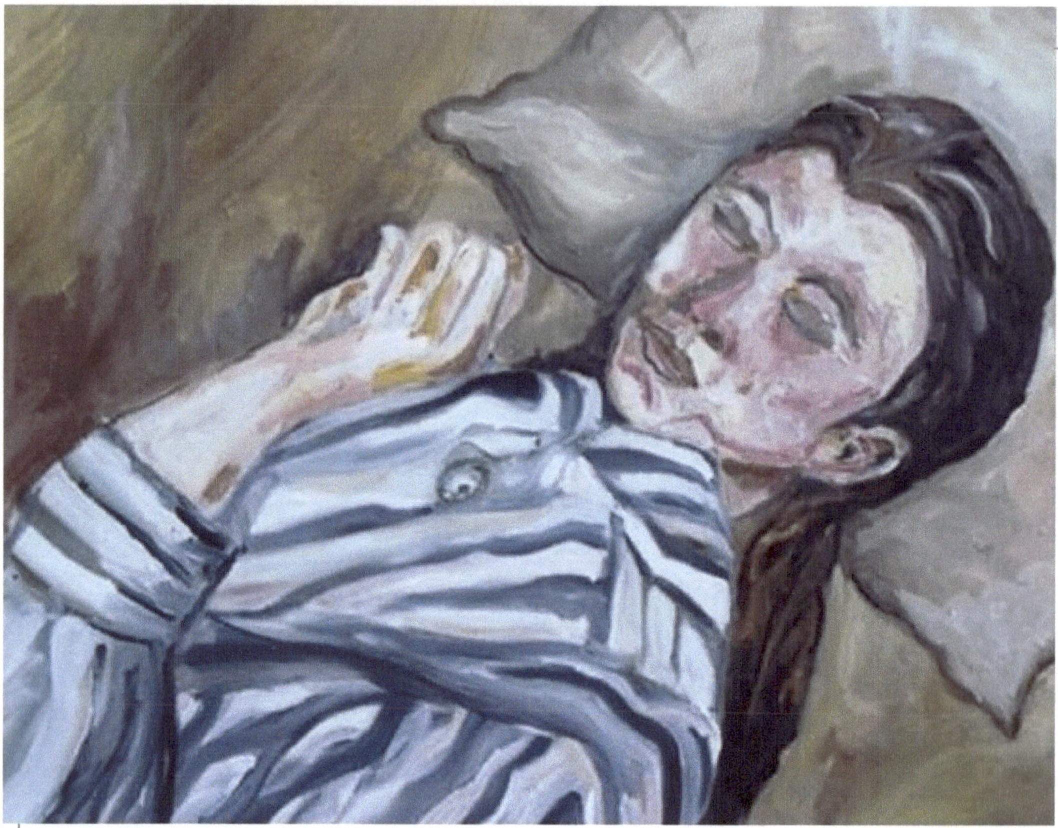

Oil on canvas, 60 by 80 cm

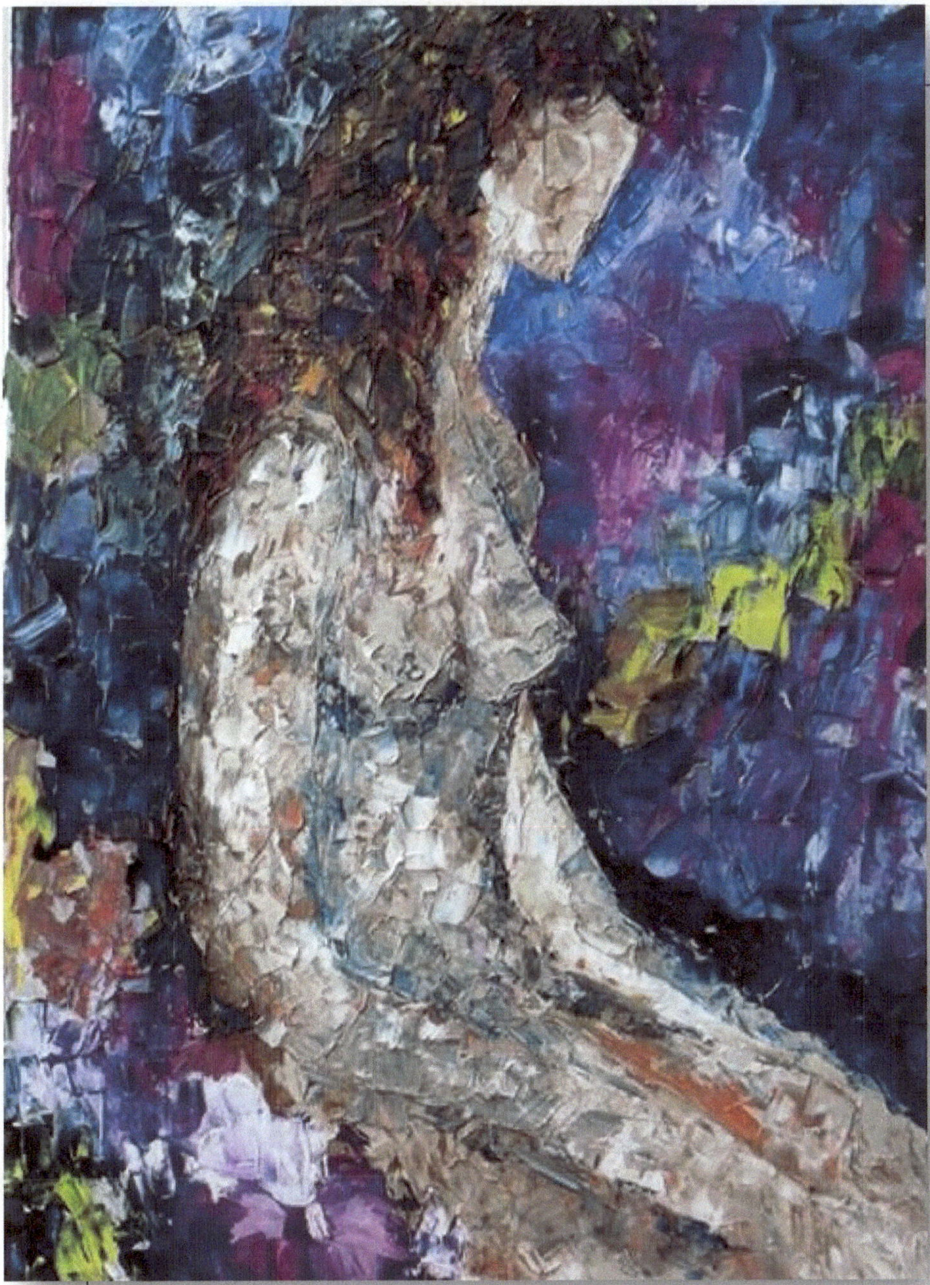

Oil on canvas, 80 by 60 cm

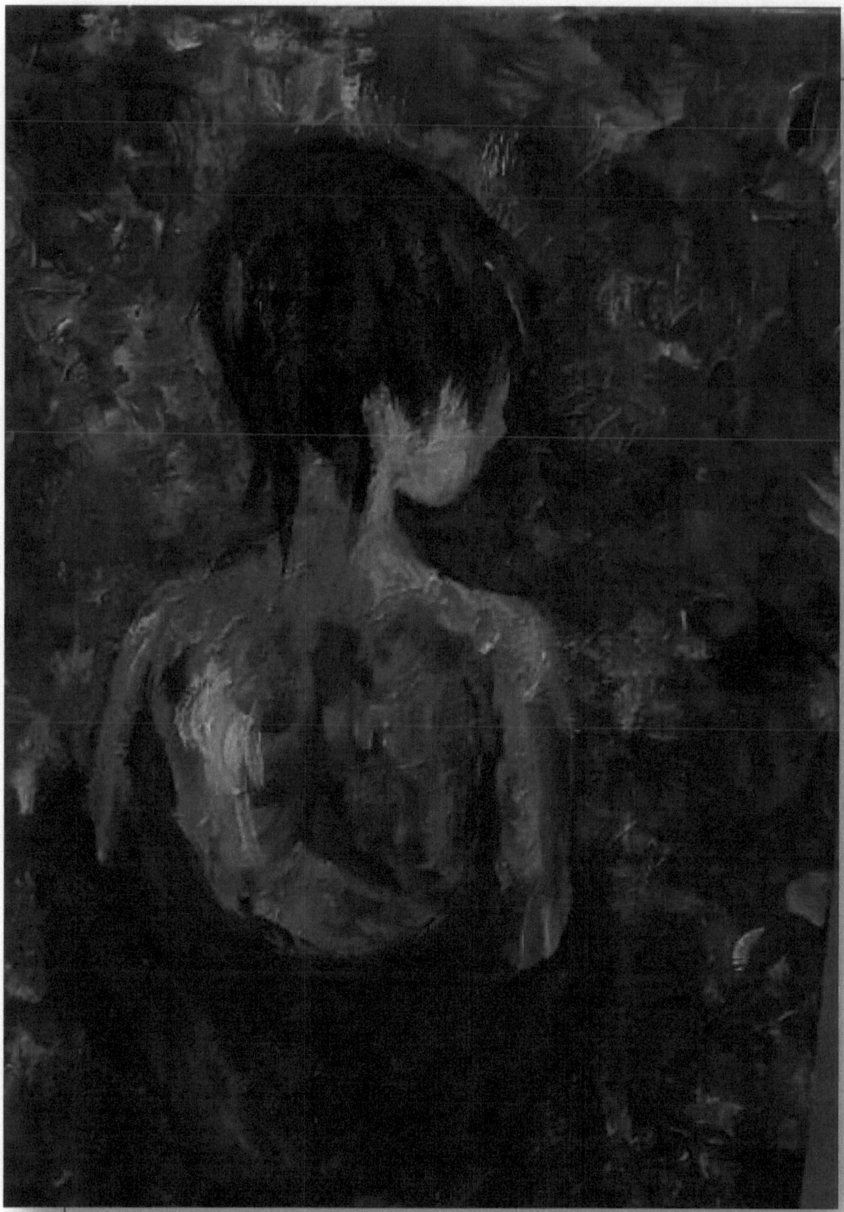

Oil on canvas, 60 by 50 cm

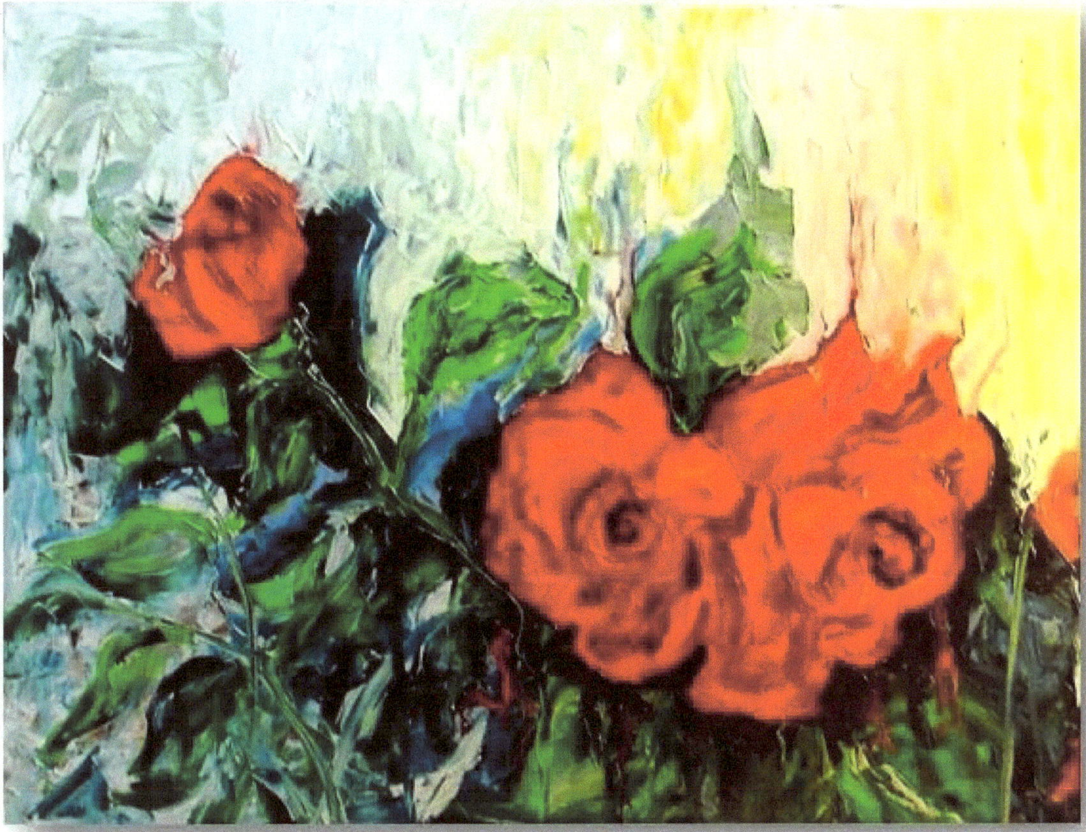

Oil on canvas, 60 by 100 cm

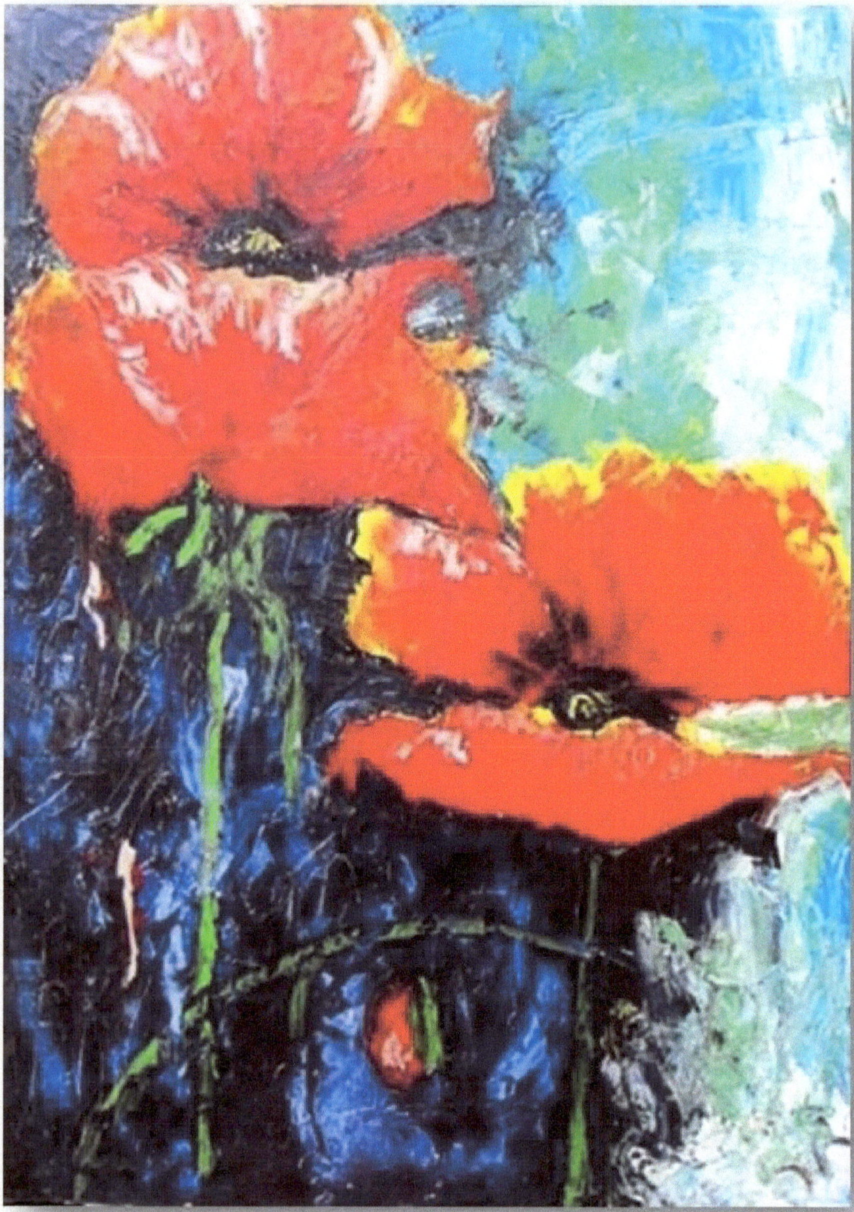

Oil on canvas, 80 by 60 cm

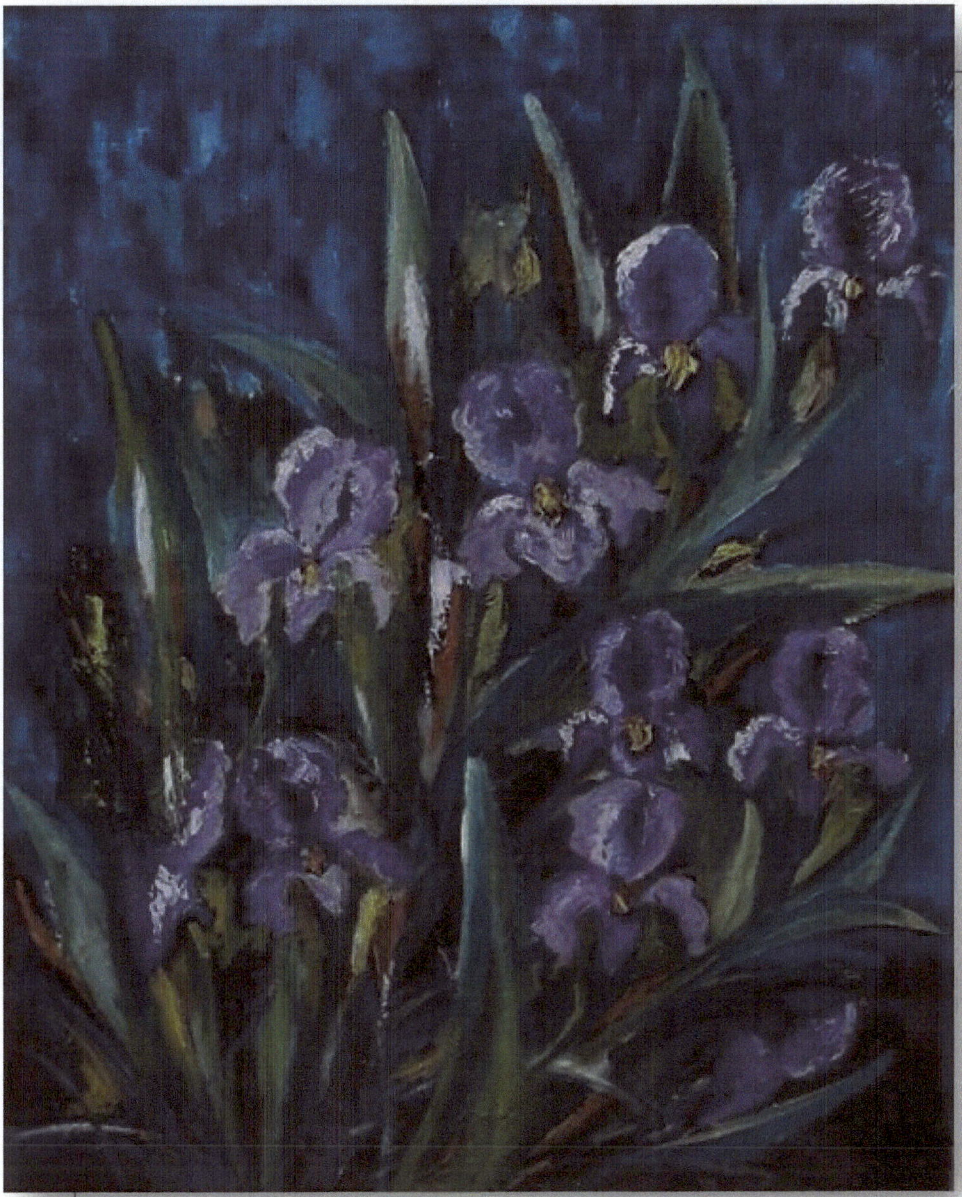

Oil on canvas, 80 by 60 cm

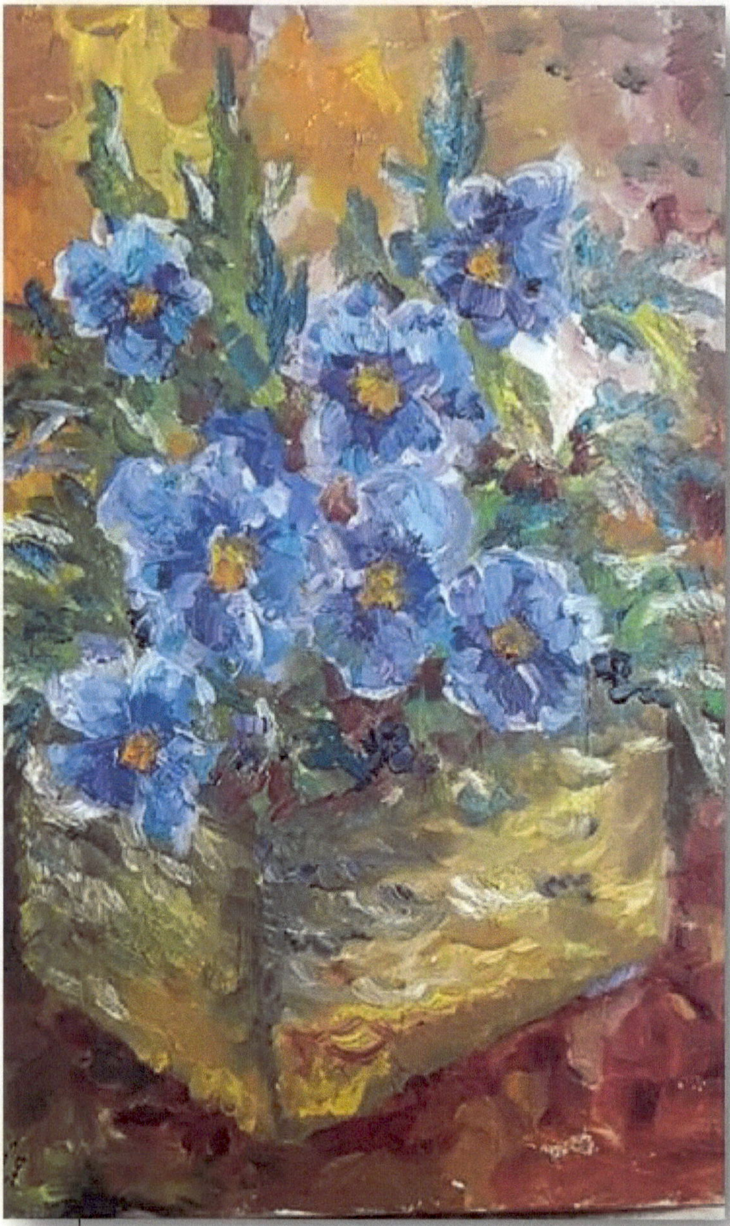

Oil on canvas, 50 by 45 cm

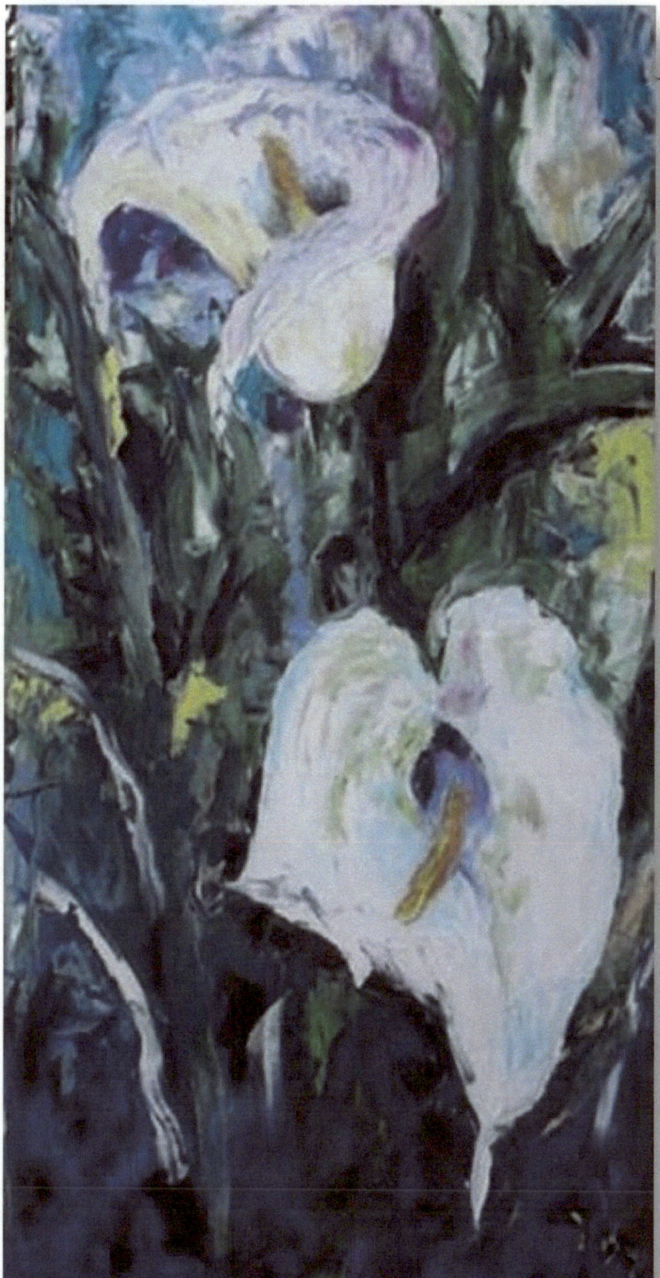

Oil on canvas, 100 by 60 cm

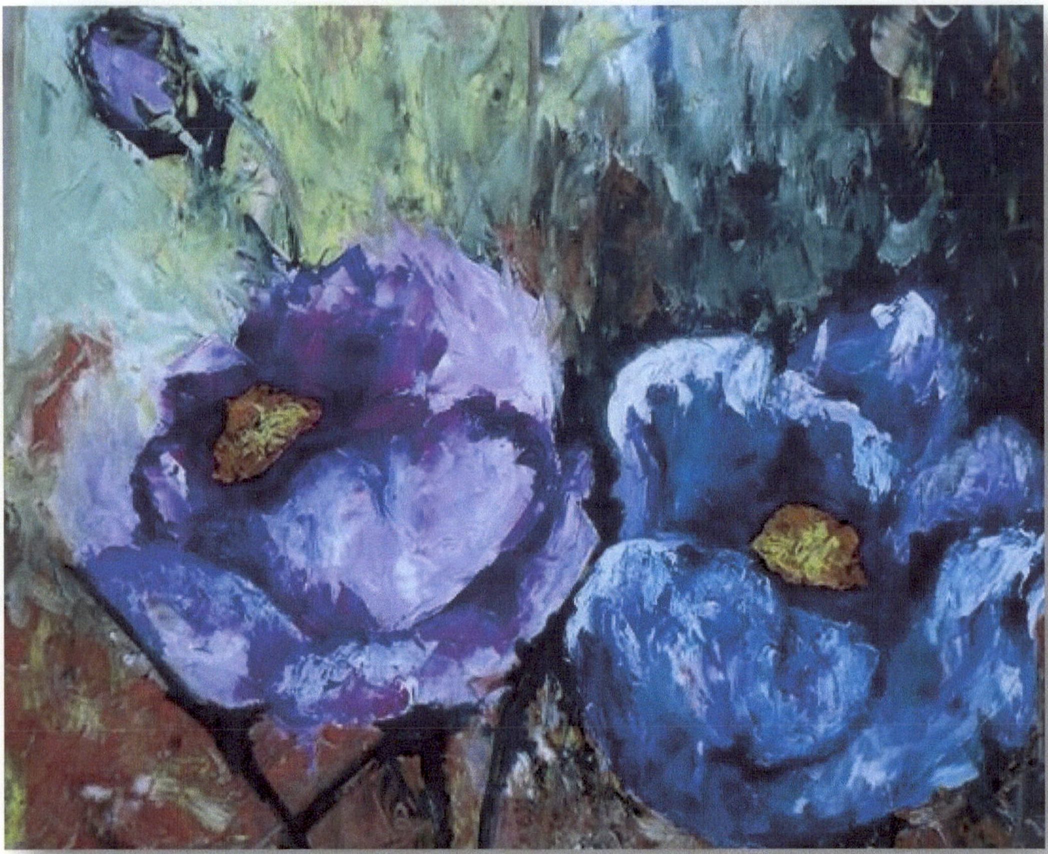

Oil on canvas, 90 by 100 cm

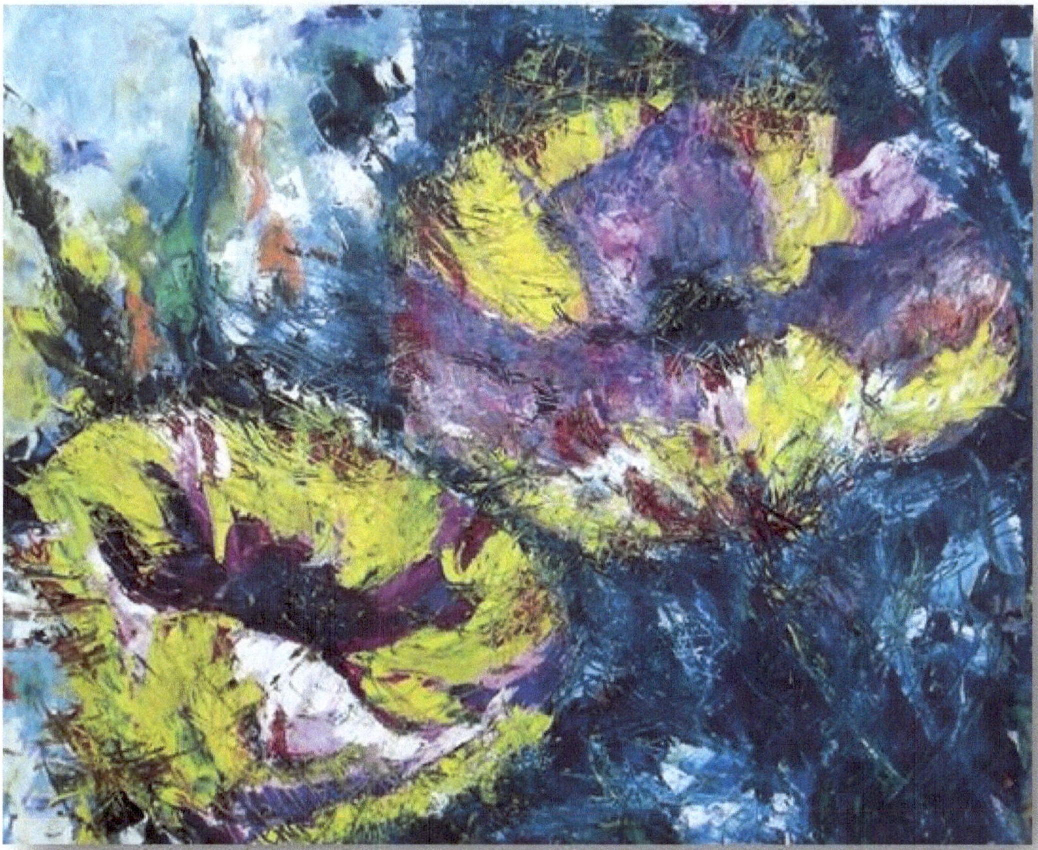

Oil on canvas, 60 by 100 cm

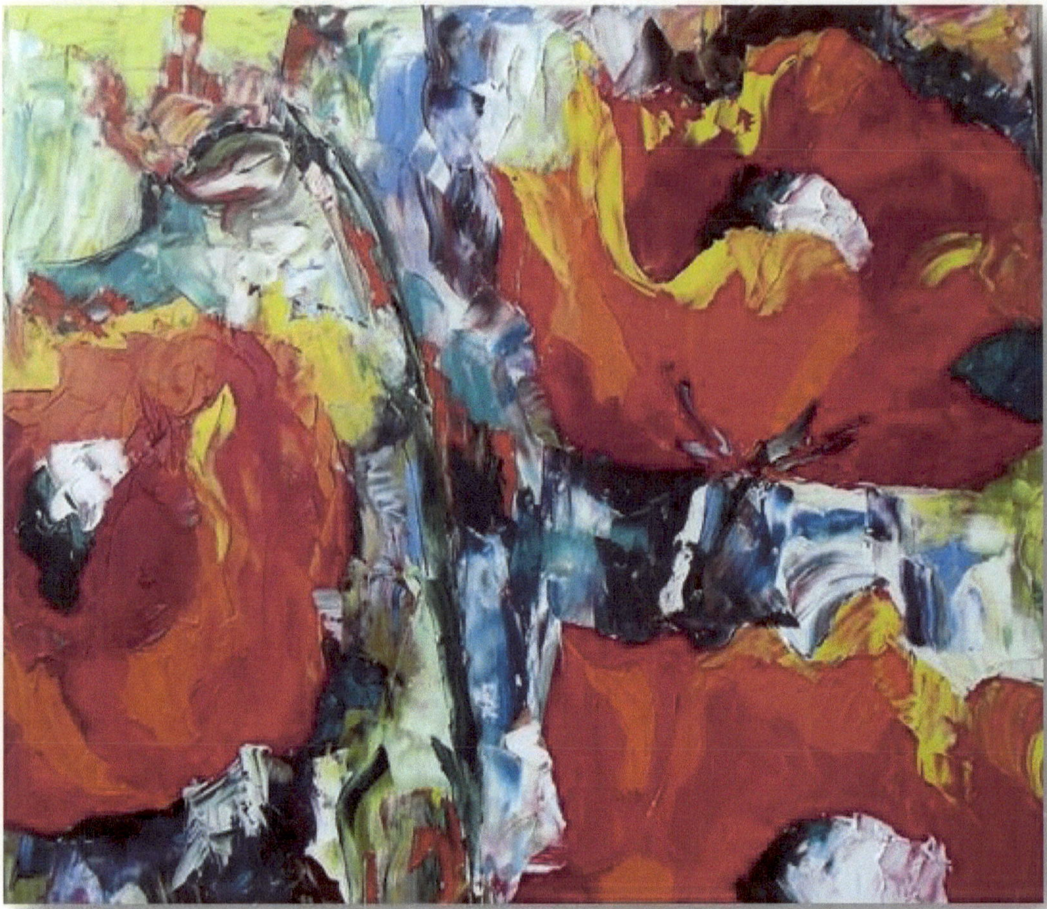

Oil on canvas, 70 by 100 cm

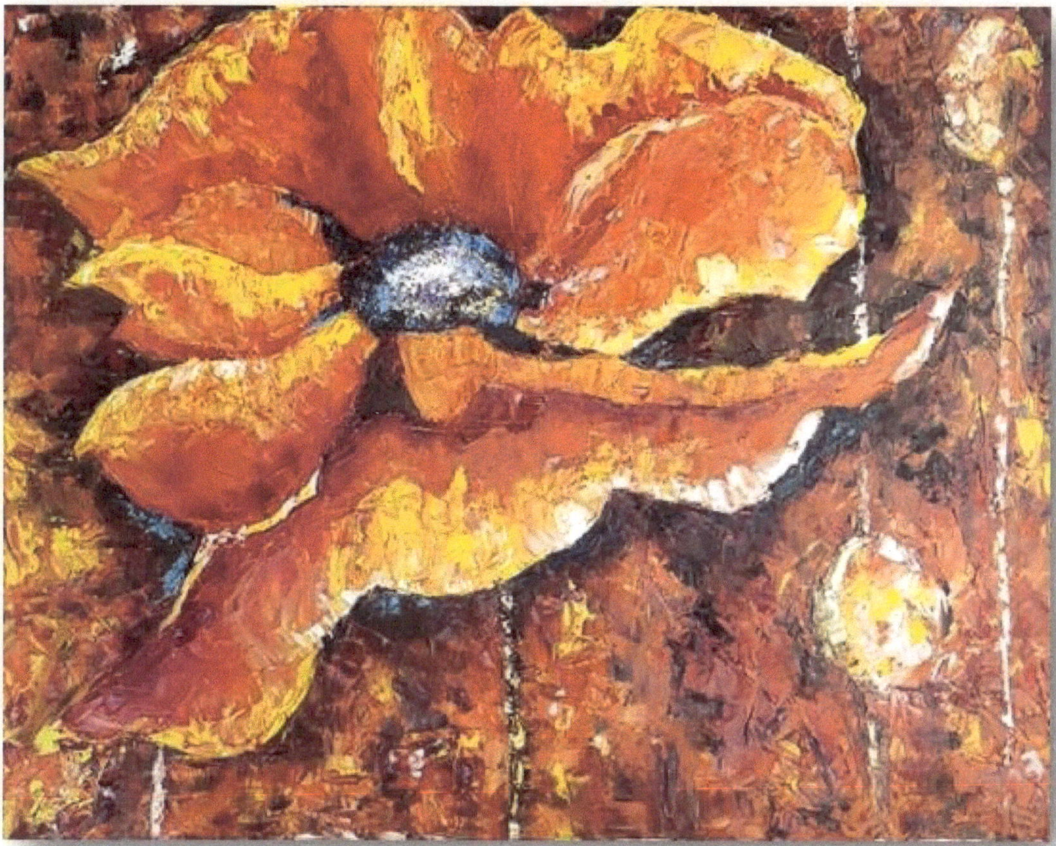

Oil on canvas, 70 by 100 cm

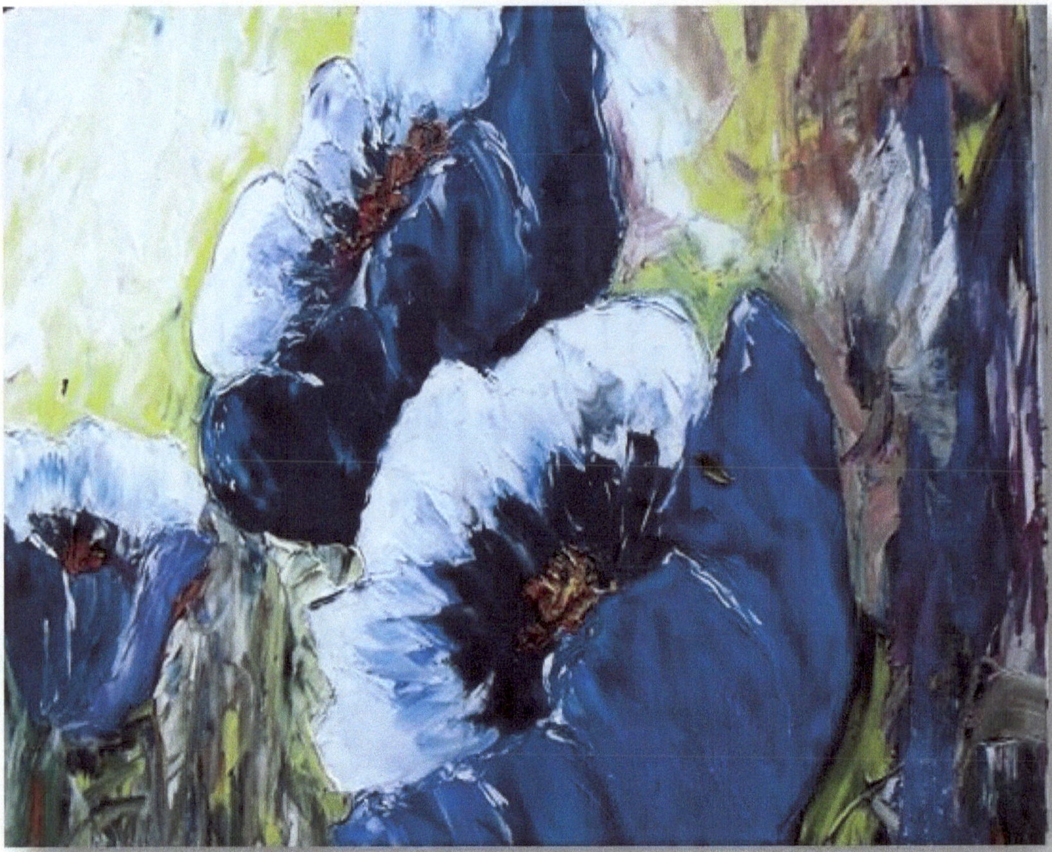

Oil on canvas, 90 by 120 cm

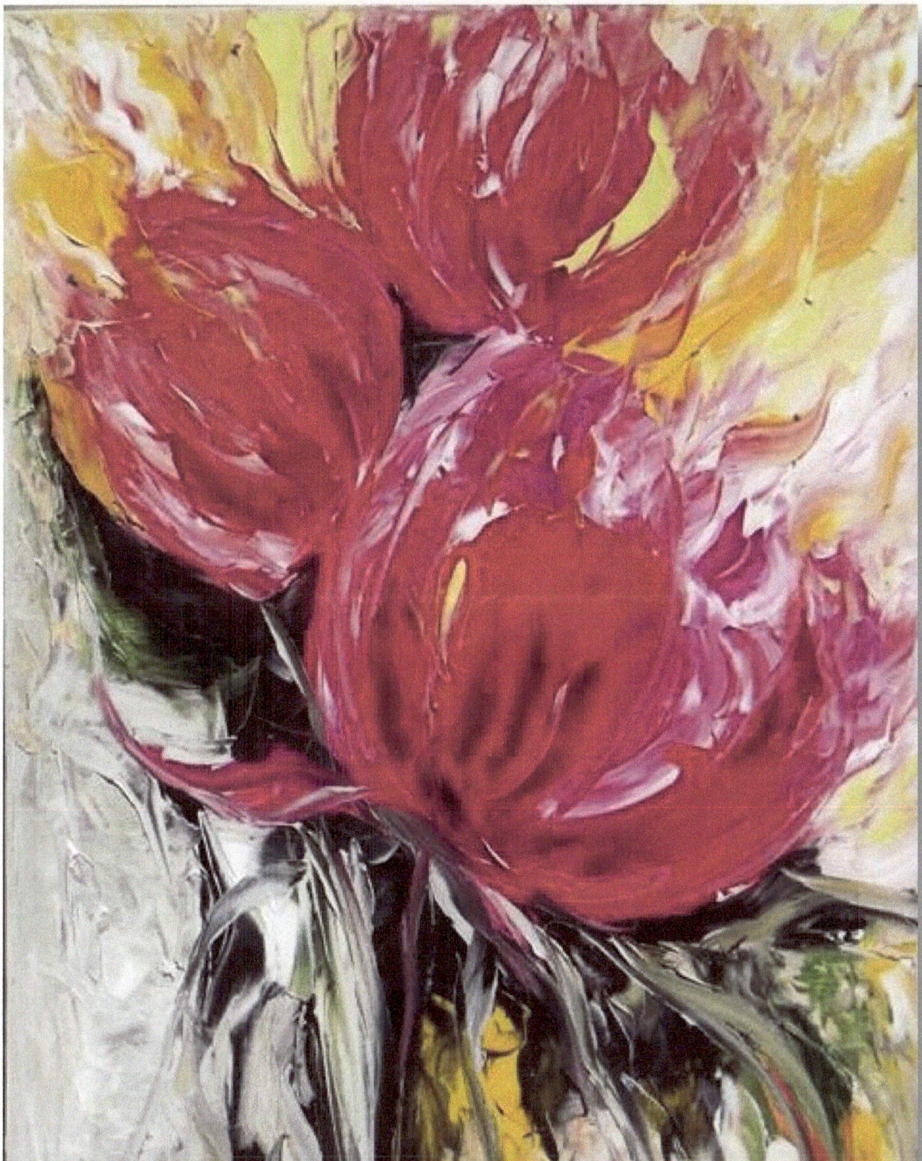

Oil on canvas, 120 by 90 cm

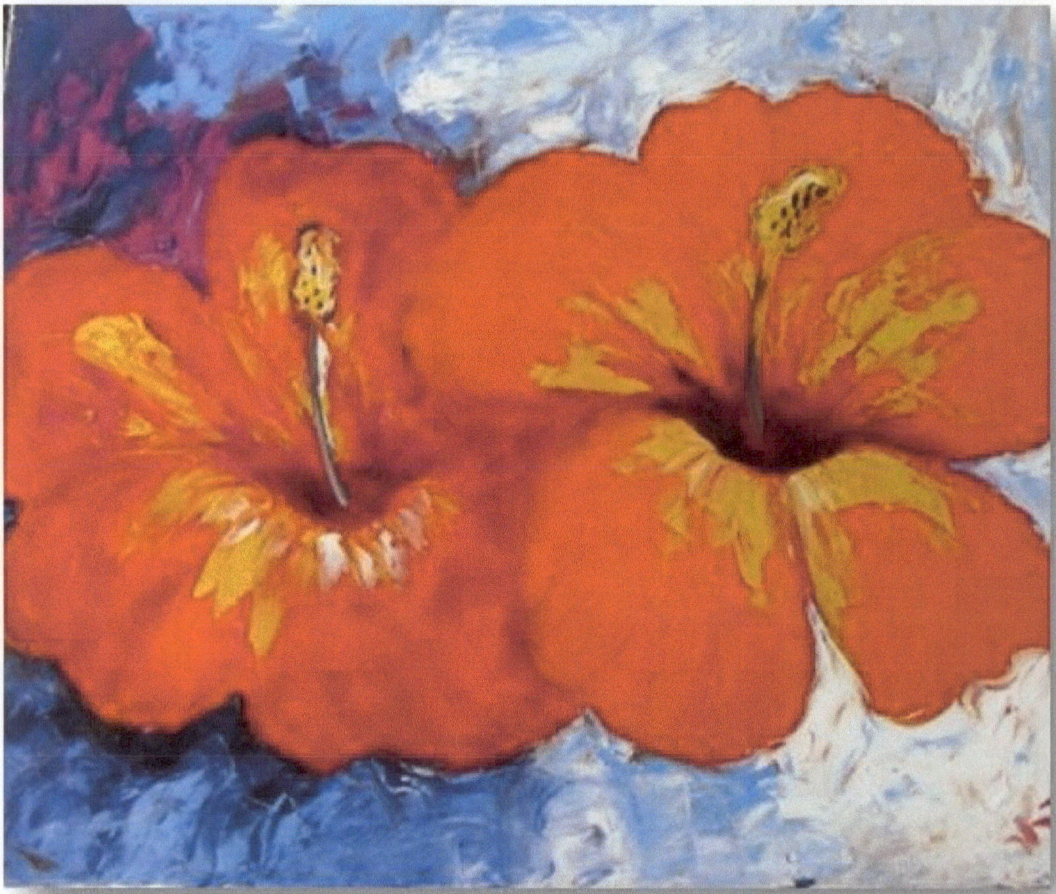

Oil on canvas, 100 by 110 cm

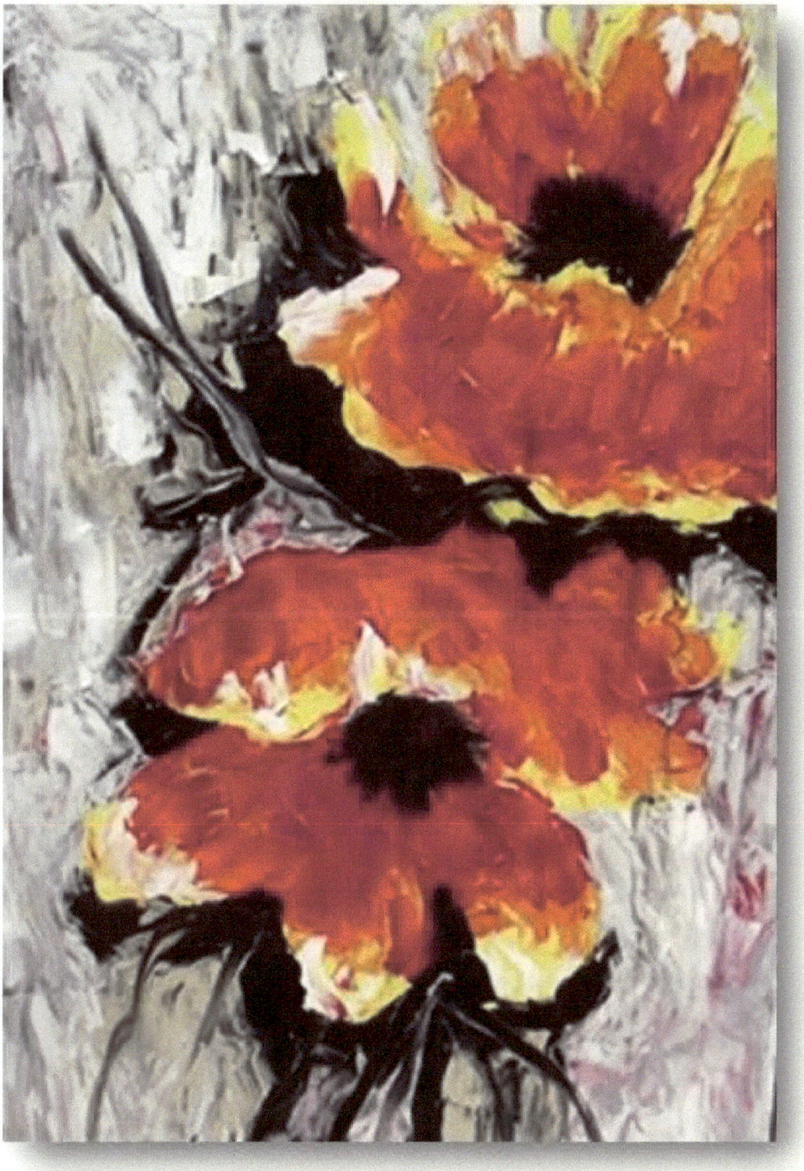

Oil on canvas, 110 by 90 cm

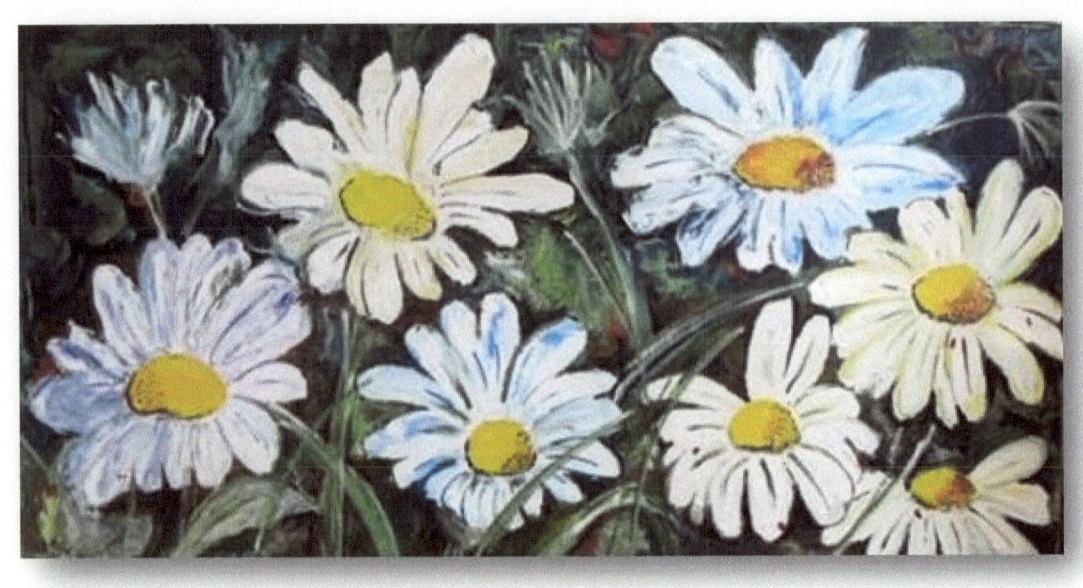

Oil on canvas, 50 by 120 cm

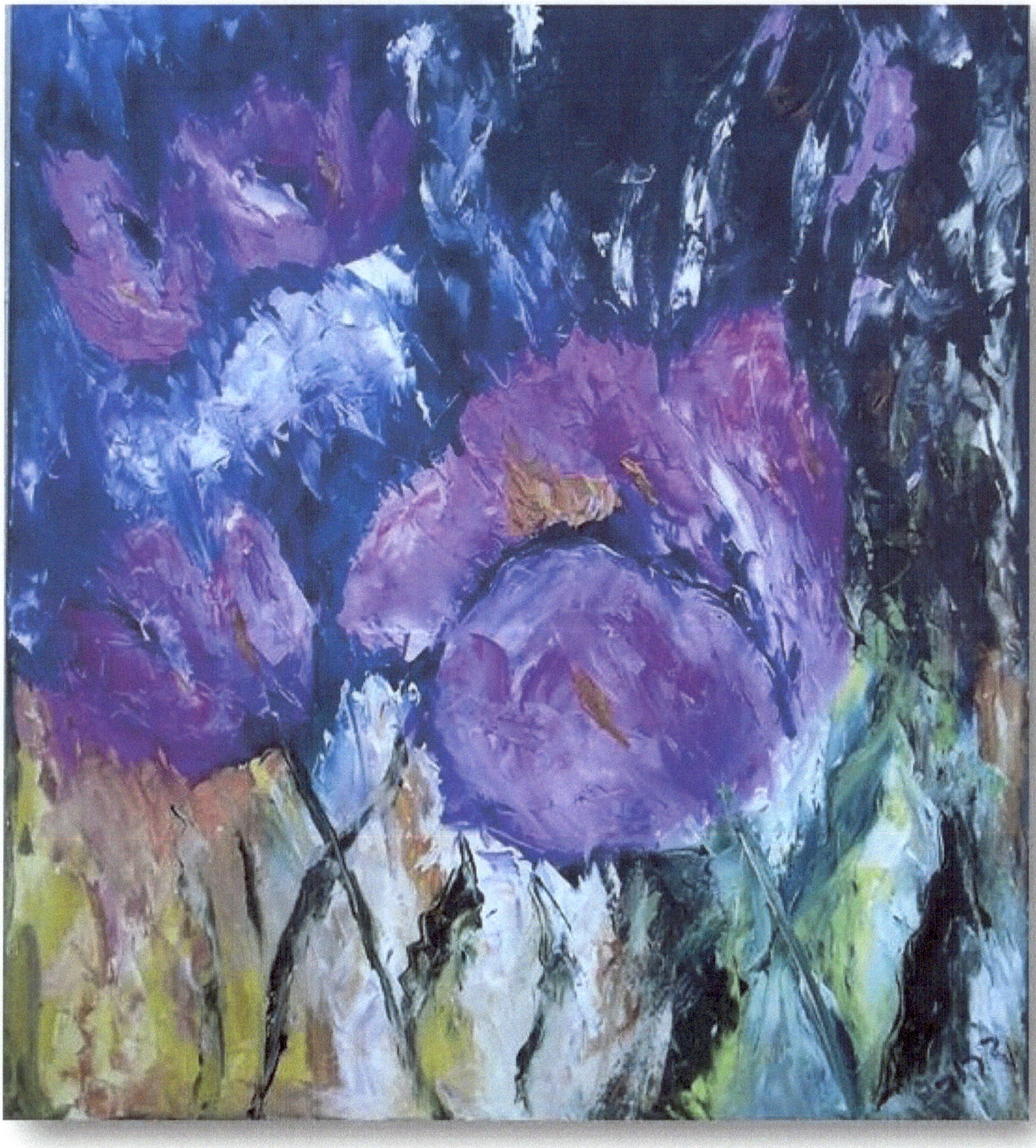

Oil on canvas, 110 by 100 cm

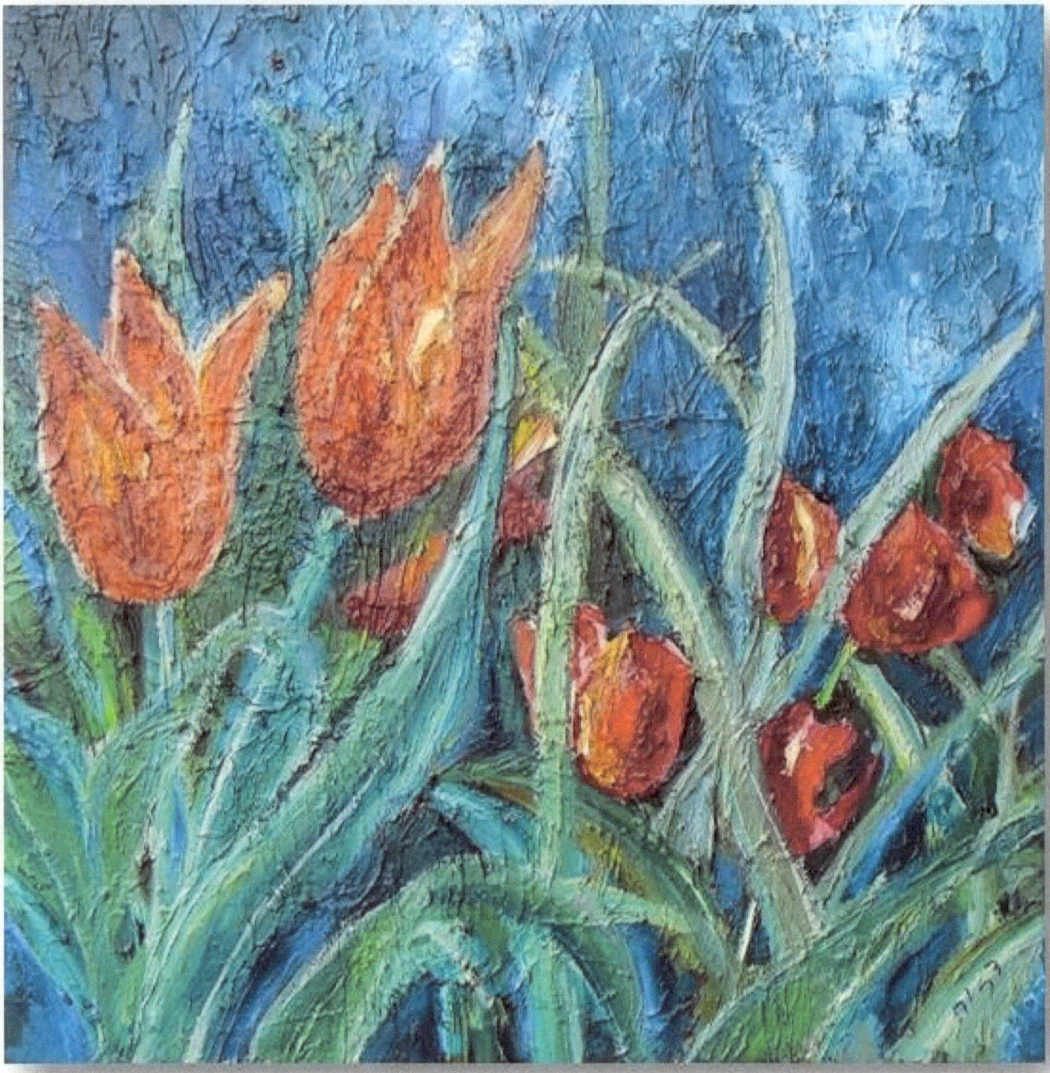

Oil on canvas, 100 by 80 cm

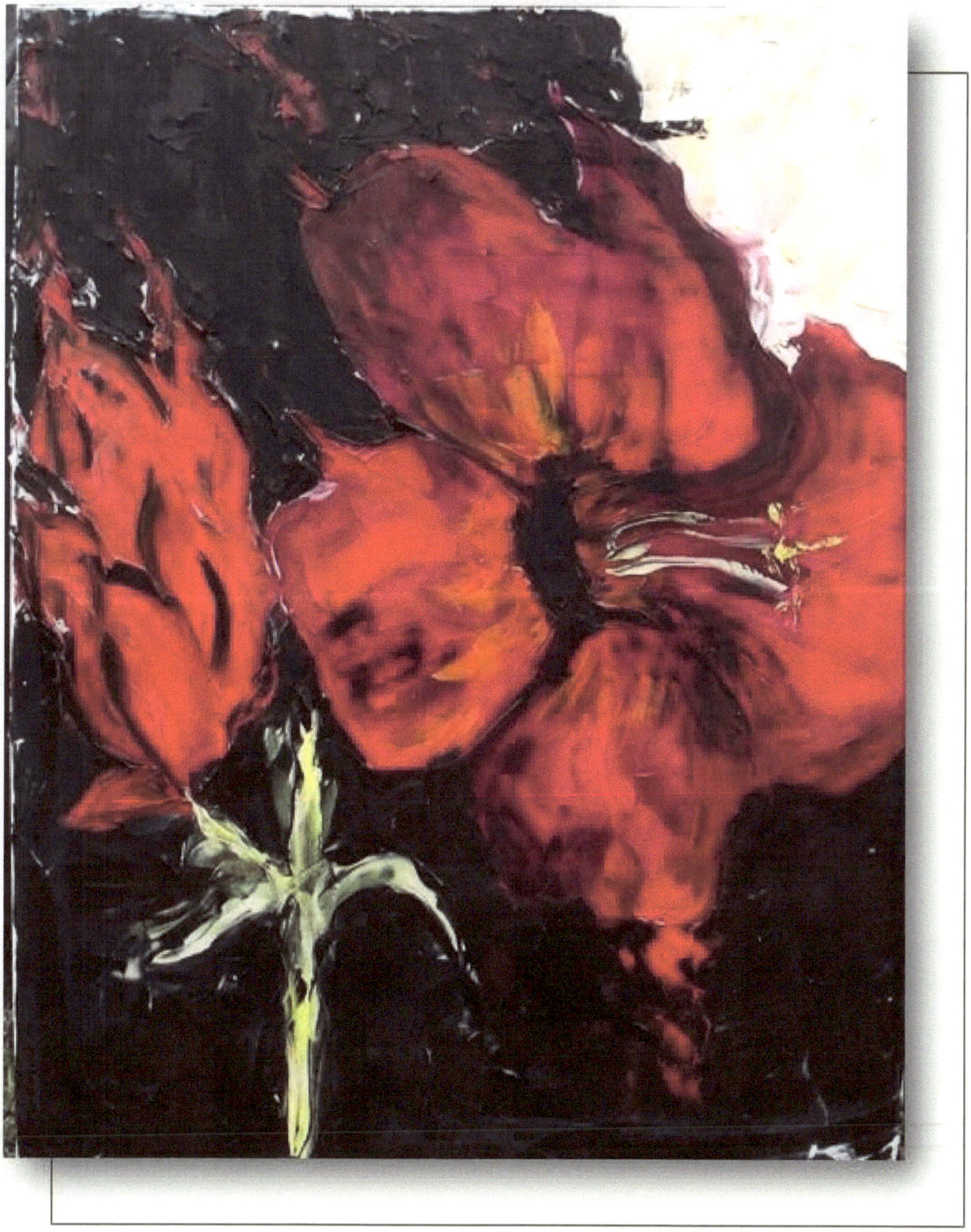

Oil on canvas, 120 by 100 cm

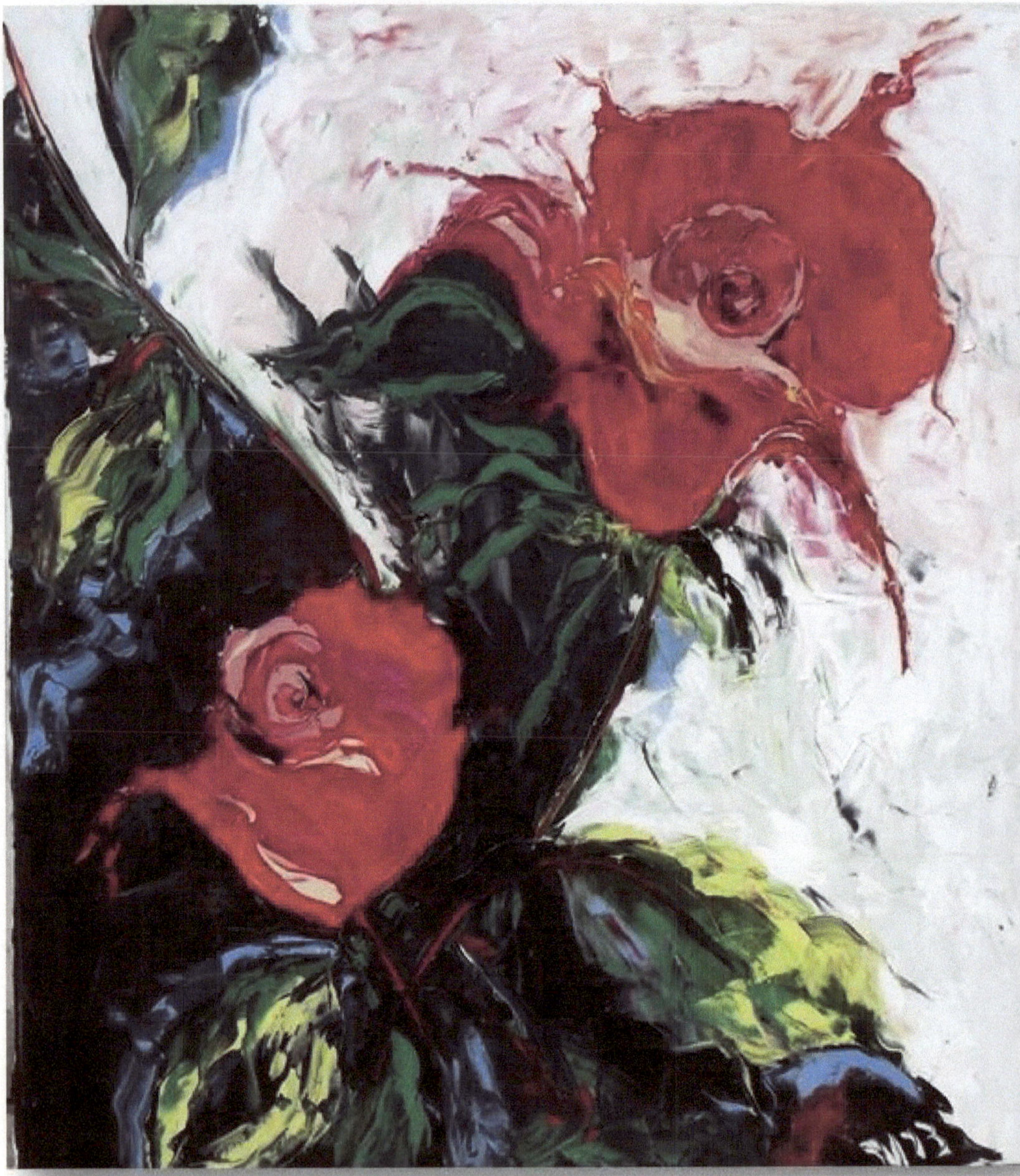

Oil on canvas, 120 by 110 cm

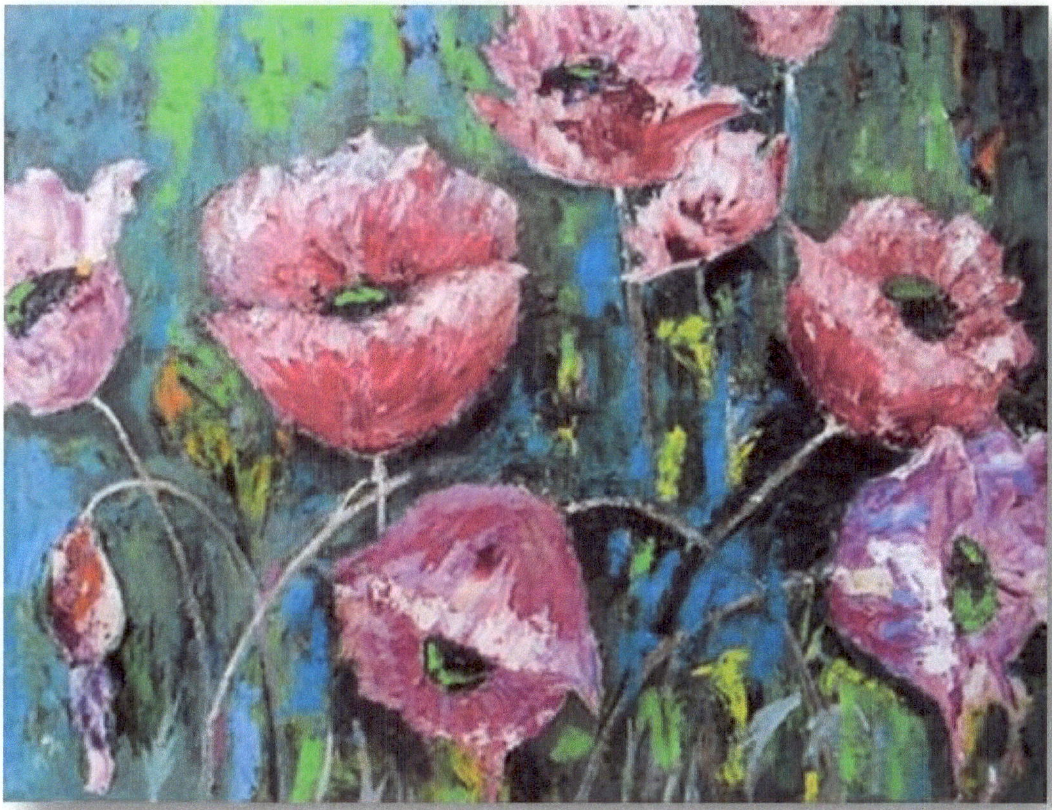

Oil on canvas, 100 by 120 cm

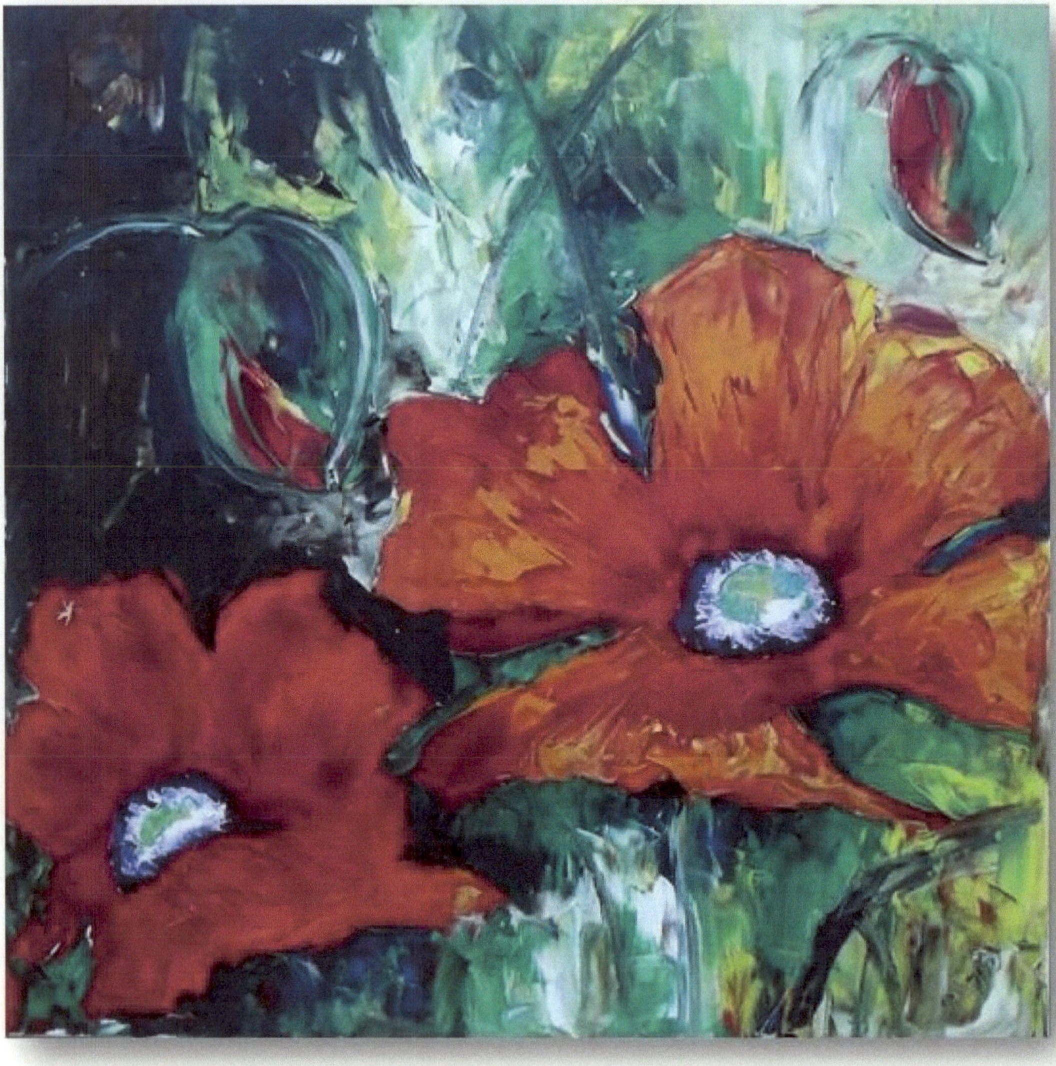

Oil on canvas, 50 by 50 cm

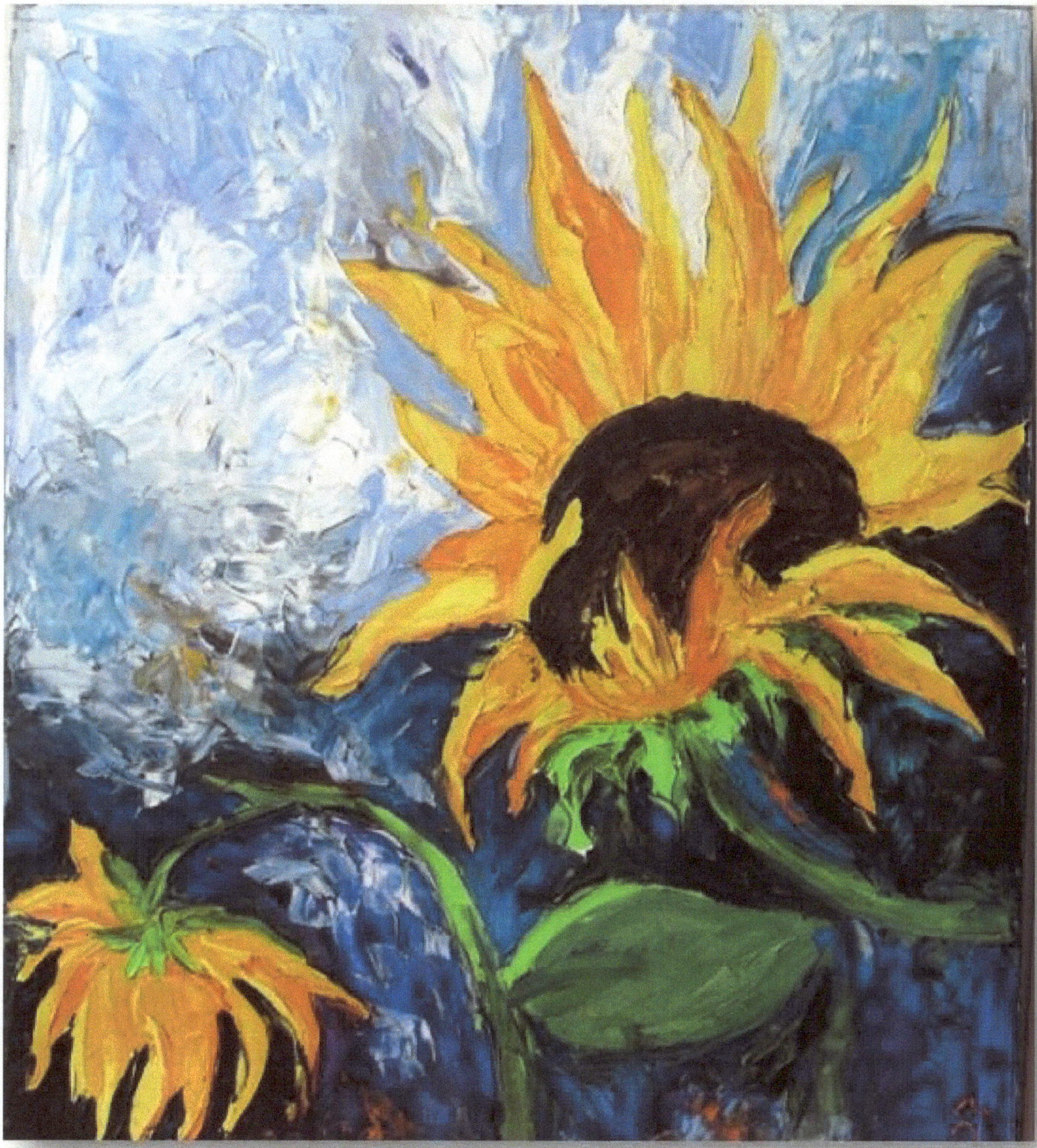

Oil on canvas, 60 by 50 cm

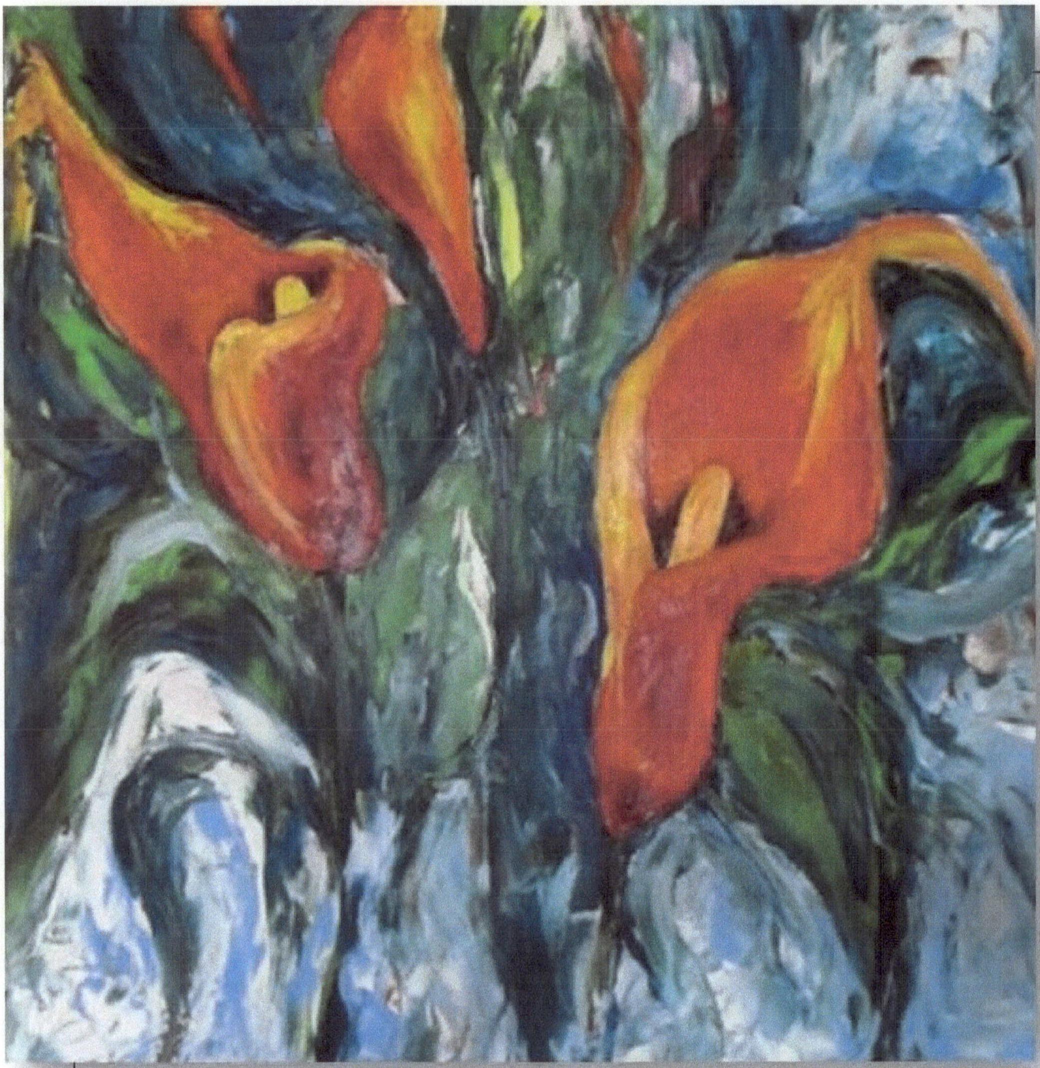

Oil on canvas, 120 by 100 cm

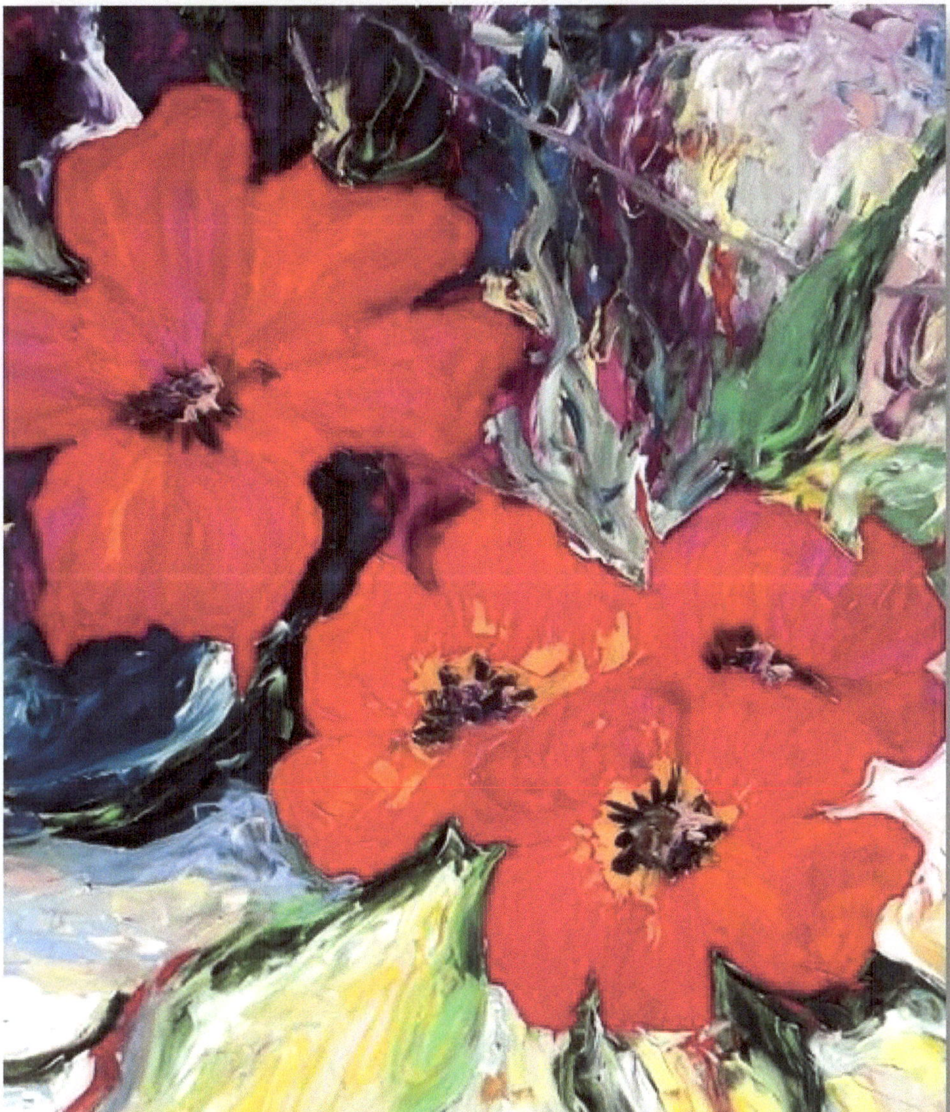

Oil on canvas, 120 by 100 cm

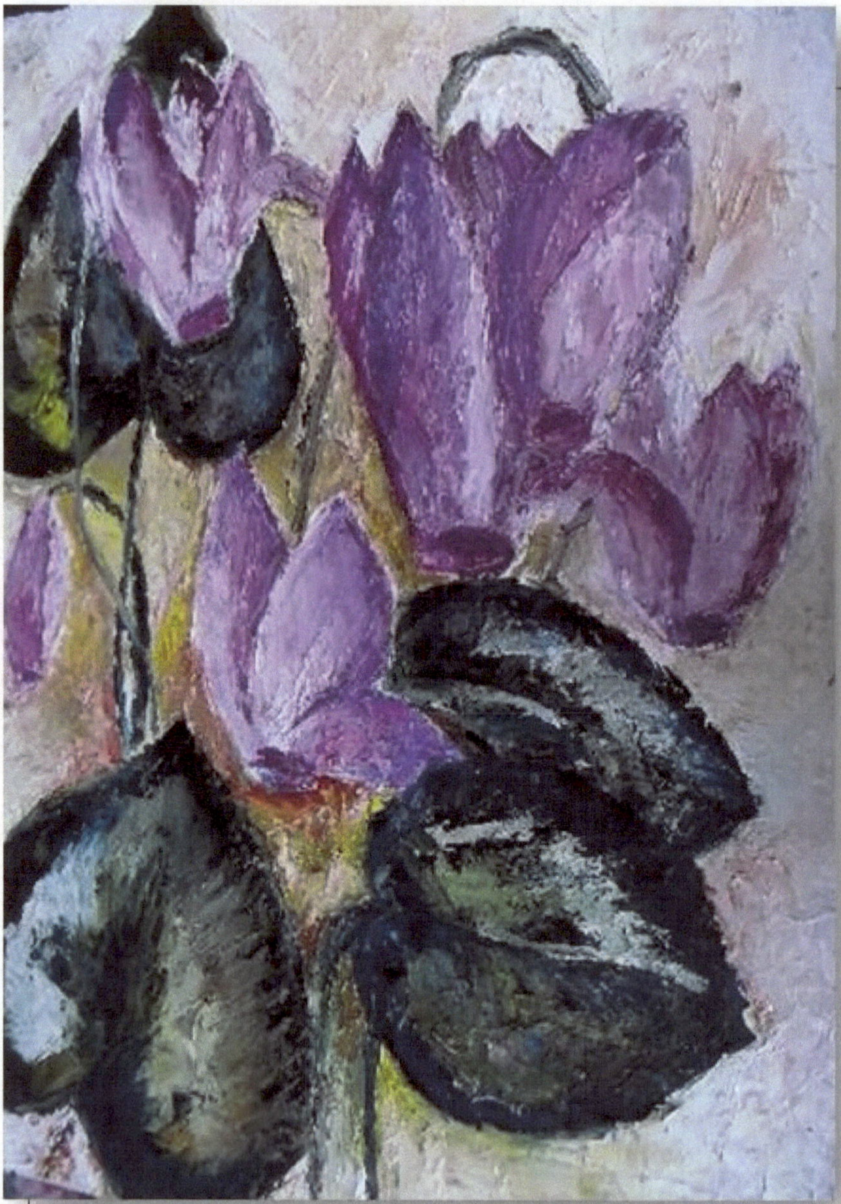

Oil on canvas, 50 by 40 cm

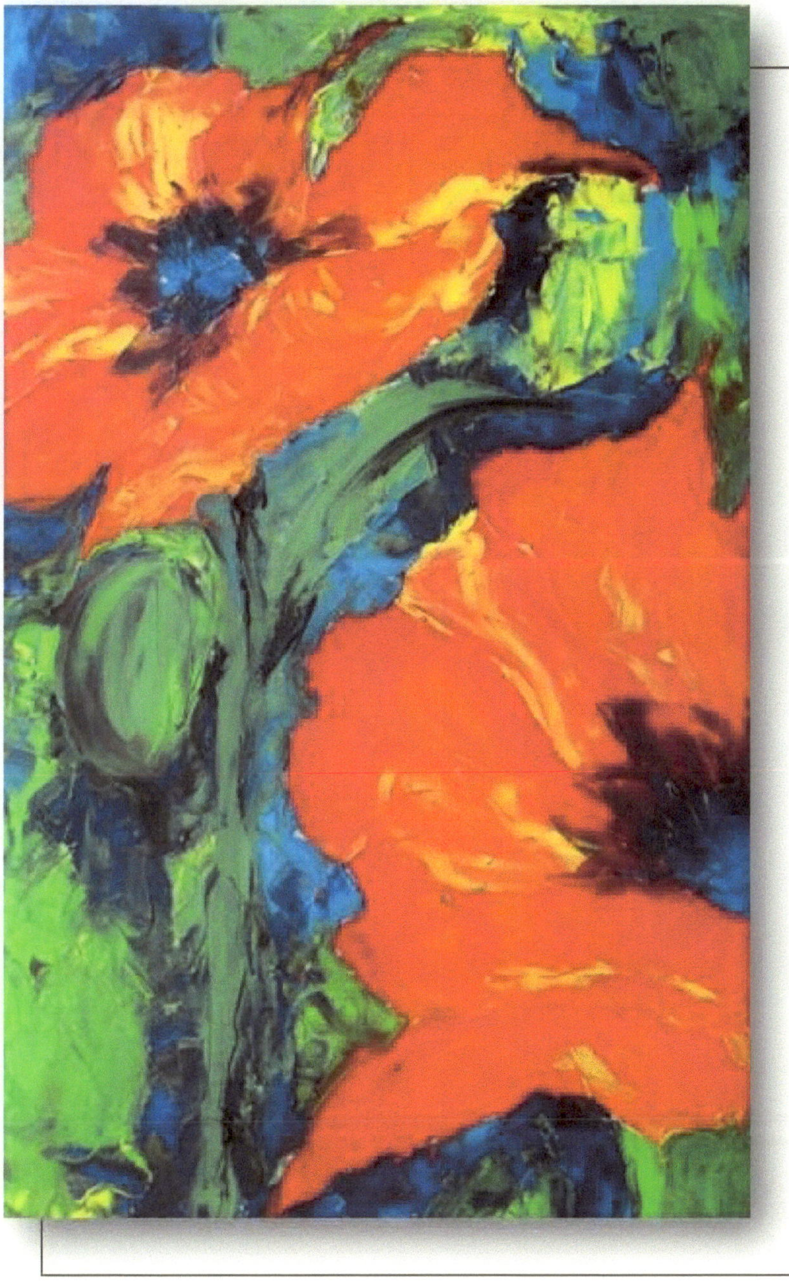

Oil on canvas, 120 by 50 cm

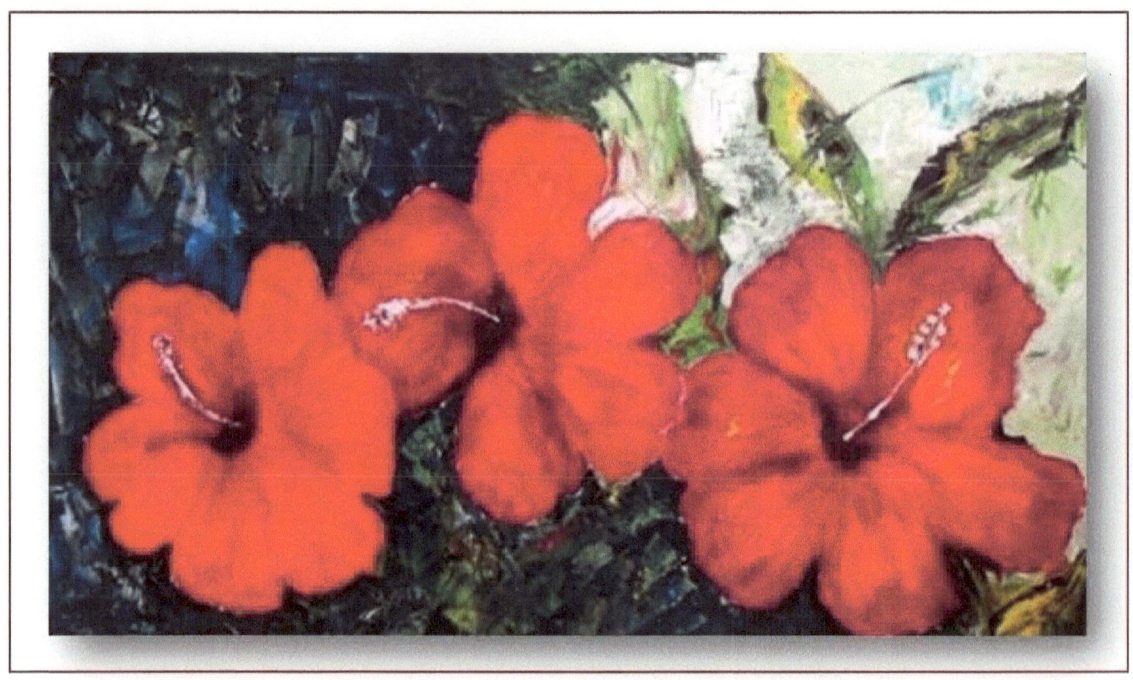

Oil on canvas, 60 by 120 cm

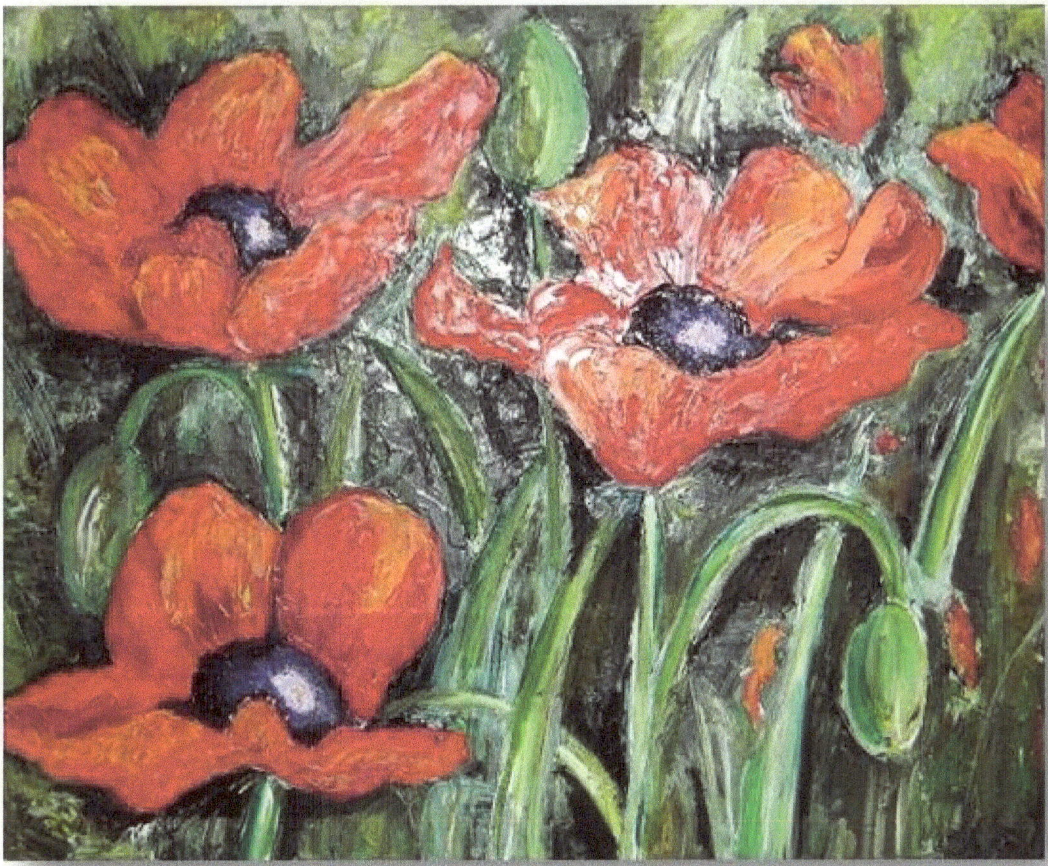

Oil on canvas, 80 by 100 cm

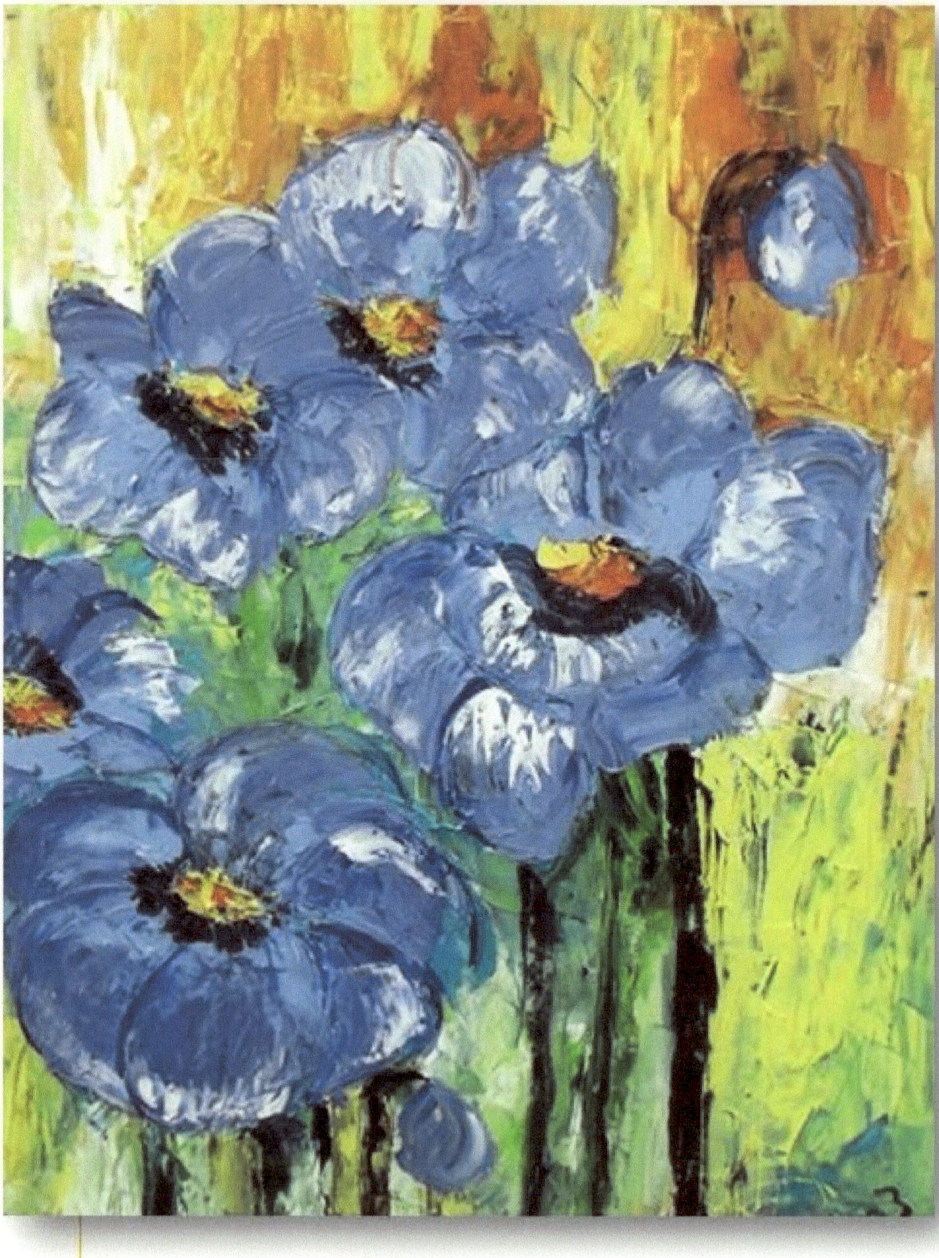

Oil on canvas, 110 by 100 cm

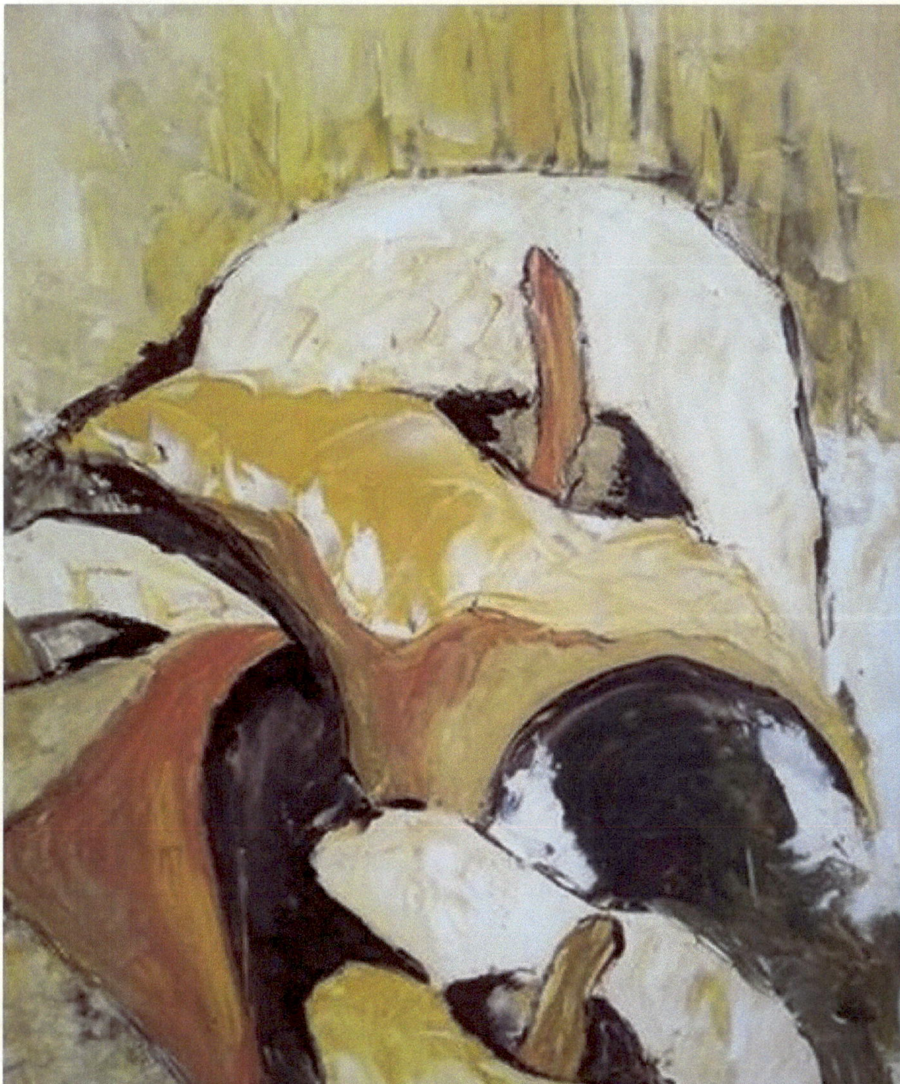

Oil on canvas, 100 by 60 cm

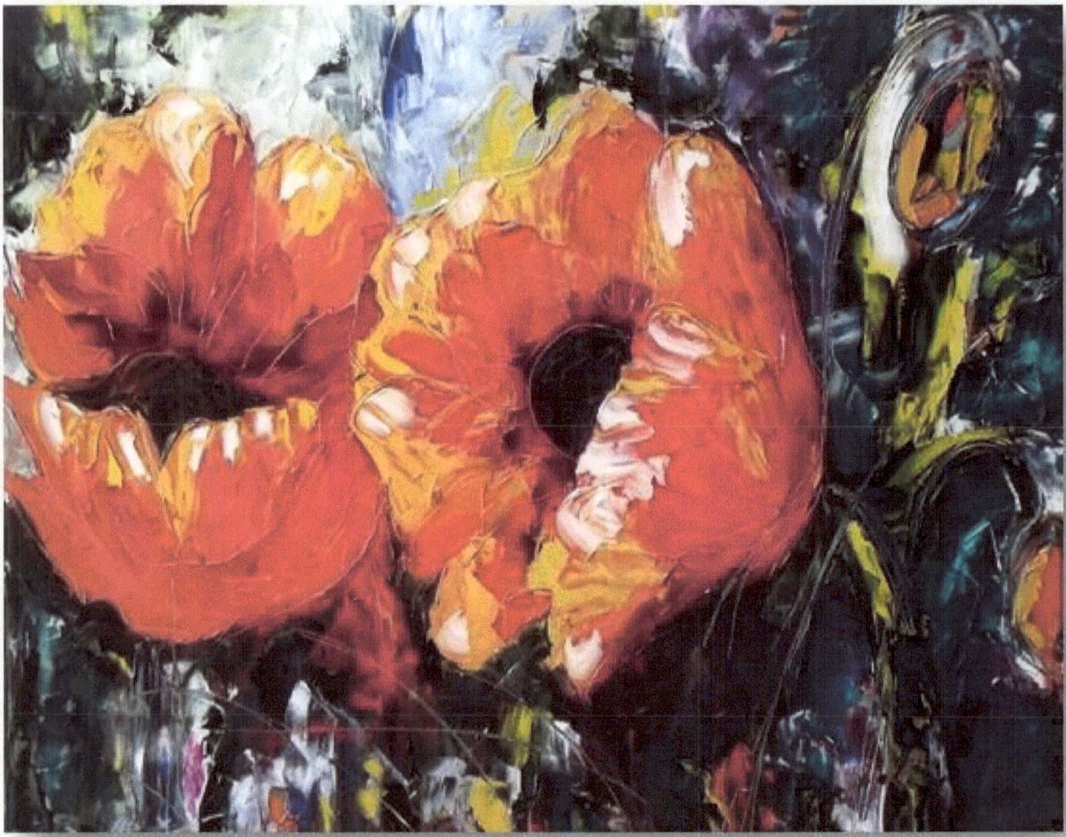

Oil on canvas, 90 by 110 cm

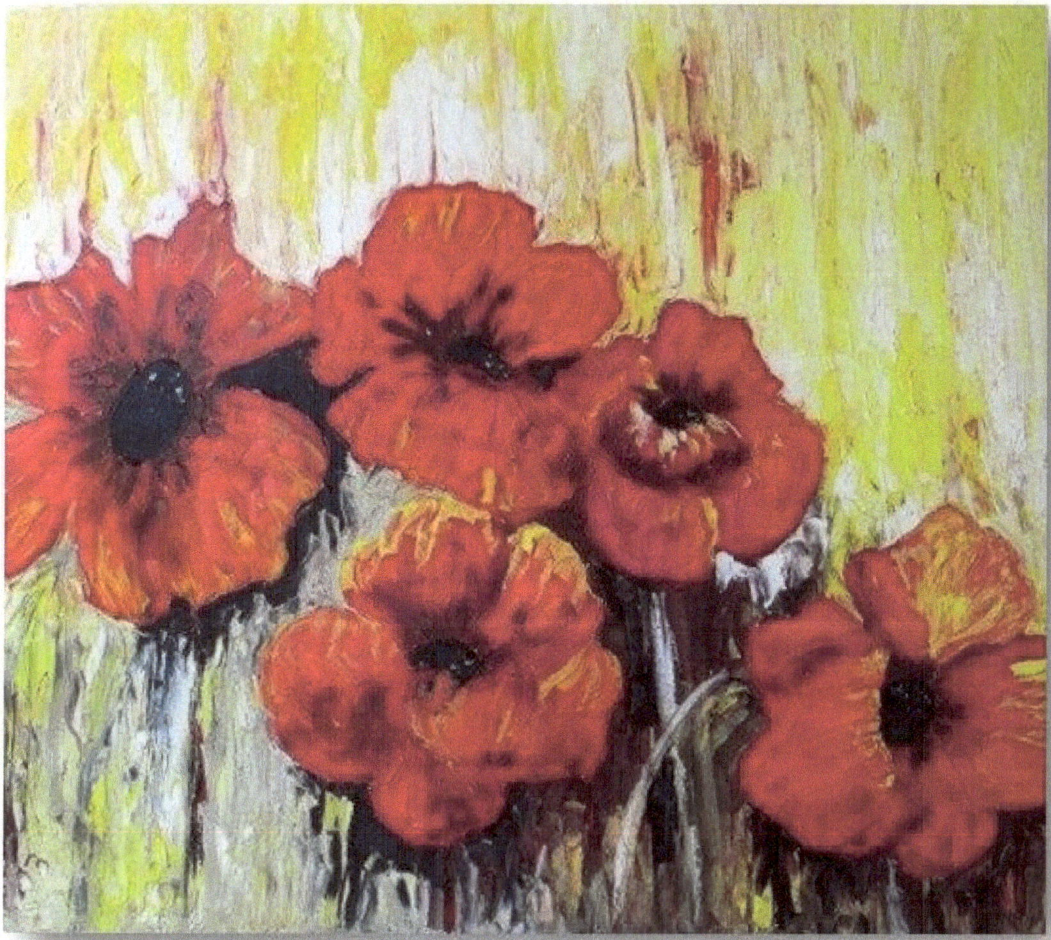

Oil on canvas, 130 by 110 cm

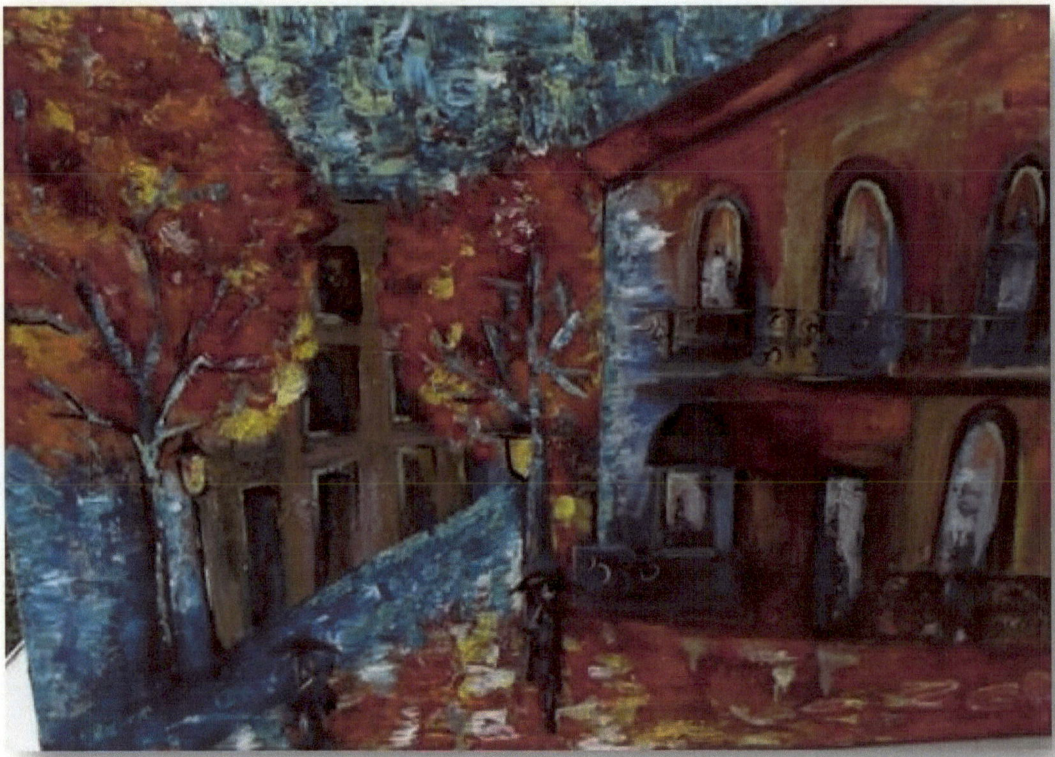

Oil on canvas, 50 by 80 cm

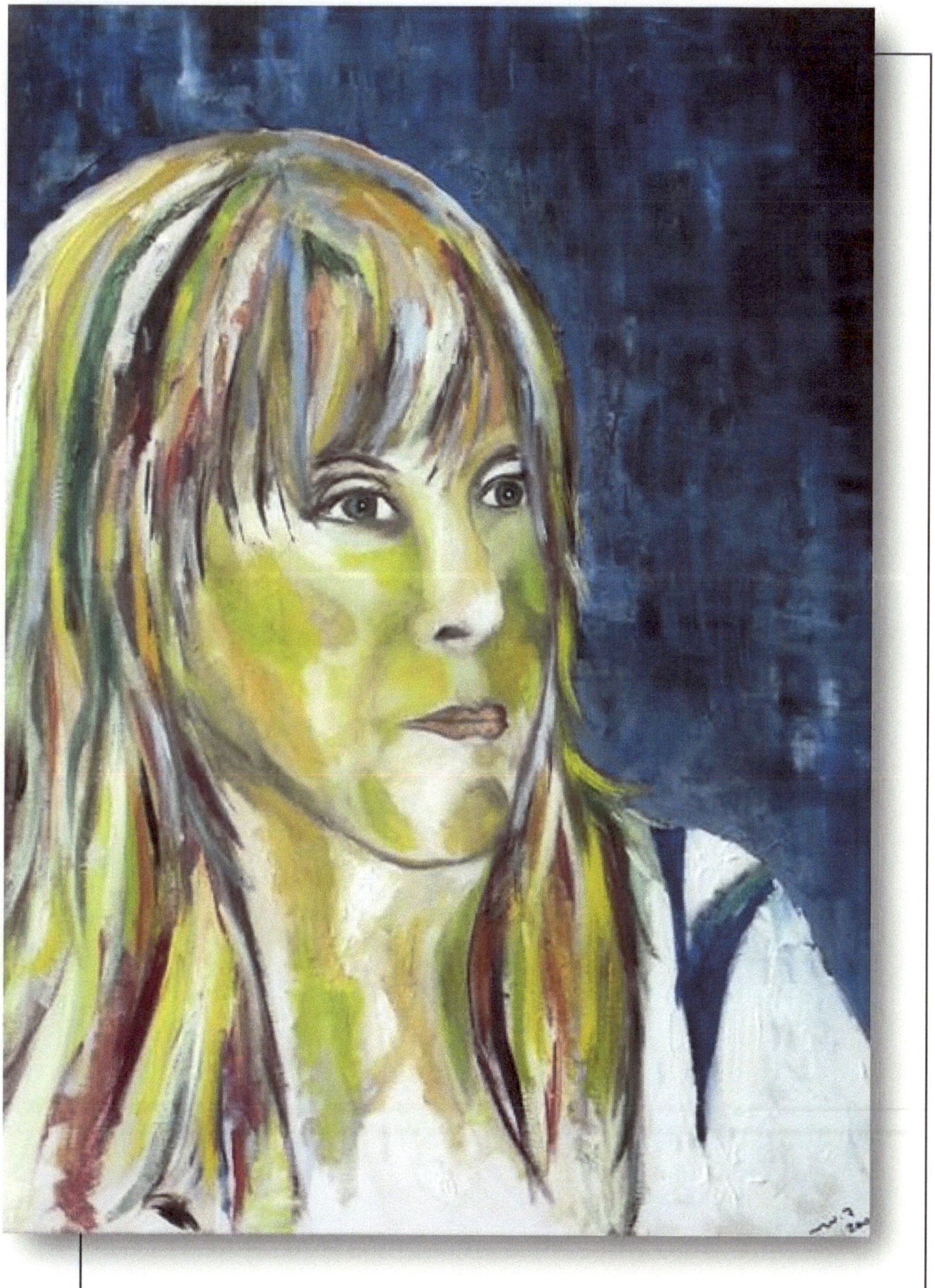

Oil on canvas, 80 by 60 cm

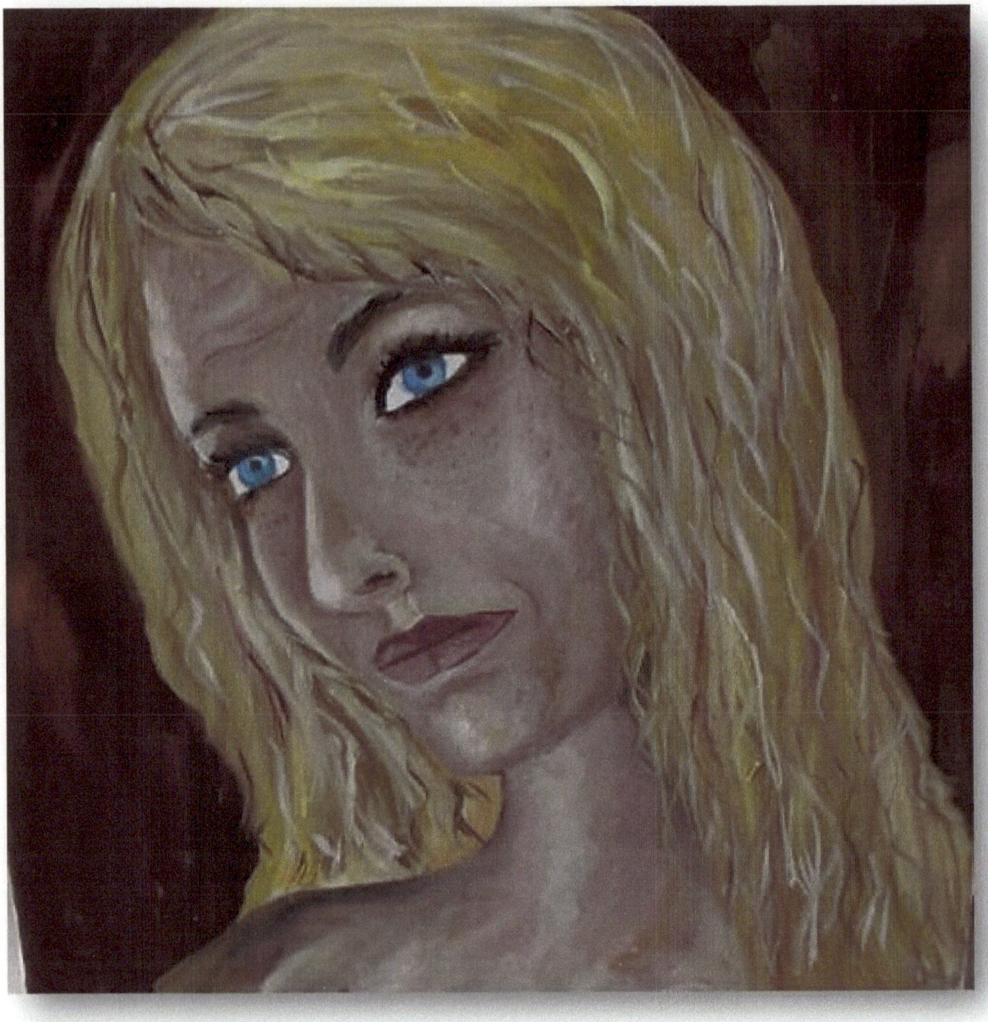

Oil on canvas, 40 by 40 cm

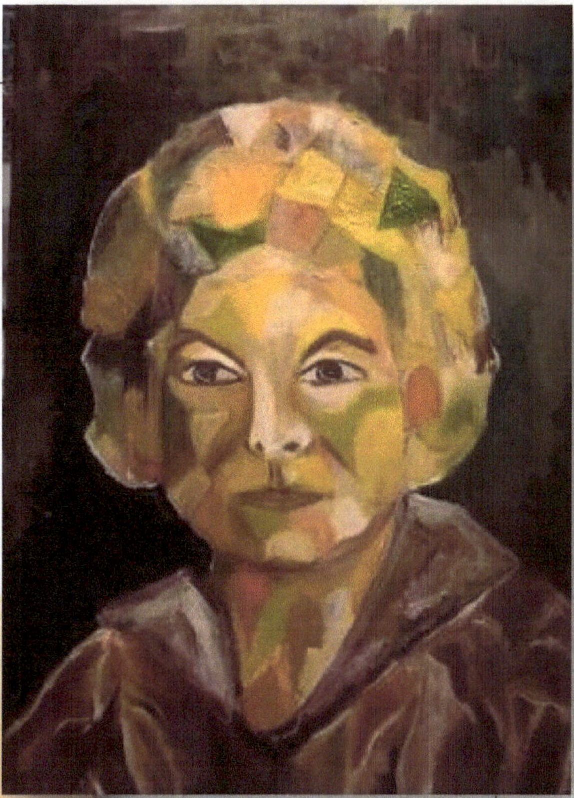

Oil on canvas, 100 by 60 cm

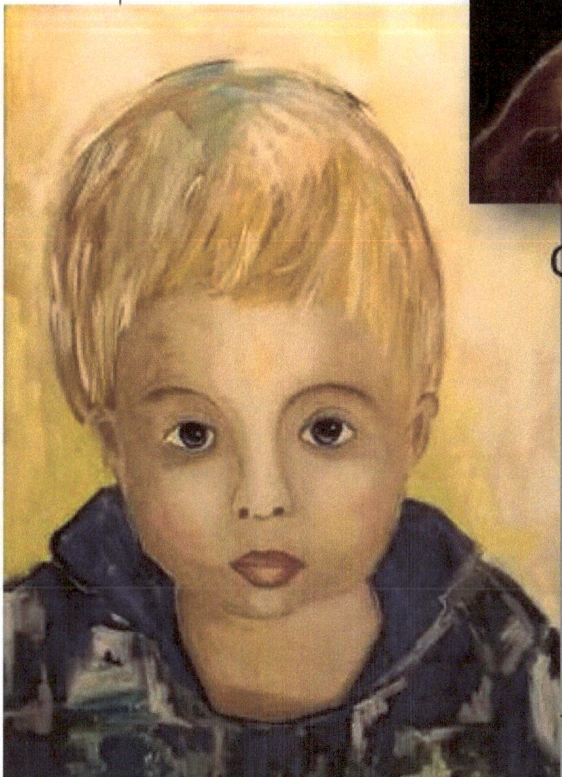

Oil on canvas, 80 by 50 cm

www.ingramcontent.com/pod-product-compliance
Lightning Source LLC
Chambersburg PA
CBHW051215220526
45473CB00003B/1040